More

Ribbon Embroidery

By Machine

More Ribbon Embroidery By Machine

Marie Duncan & Betty Farrell

krause
publications

700 E. State Street • Iola, WI 54990-0001

Library of Congress Cataloging-in-Publication Data

Duncan, Marie.
    More Ribbon Embroidery By Machine / Marie Duncan and Betty Farrell
    p.96   cm.
    ISBN 0-8019-9047-5
      1. Silk ribbon embroidery. 2. Embroidery,
    Machine. 3.Embroidery, Machine -
    Patterns. I. Farrell, Betty. II. Title.

                                        97-073026
                                        CIP

CONTENTS

Resources

Part Three:
The Projects

INTRODUCTION

"Help! We're being swallowed by a sea of silk ribbon! What a way to go!"

More Ribbon Embroidery by Machine is a follow up to **Ribbon Embroidery by Machine**, published by Chilton; a division of Krause Publications in the fall of 1996. Before finishing, we were bursting with ideas for more projects. In this book, we present details of specific stitches, colors and instructions for you to recreate each project. The ideas keep flowing from our imaginations; all we need is time to execute and put them on paper.

We offer machine ribbon embroidery to everyone!

Being total machine enthusiasts, we developed techniques for doing stitches that have been, traditionally, done by hand. Machine techniques offer unlimited possibilities and a whole new art form! Some people feel they can embroider more quickly by hand. Initially machine embroidery may be slow, but like any new skill, one must master the learning curve. After which, the work goes faster.

In **Ribbon Embroidery by Machine**, we introduced you to basic stitches and expanded them into flowers, pots, baskets and projects. **More Ribbon Embroidery by Machine** will enable you to put to use your newly acquired talents.

We will take you into a whole new world of projects which combine ribbon embroidery with a variety of techniques. Information and techniques include beading by machine, boiled wool, heirloom sewing, applique', machine embroidery, decorative effects, bobbin thread embroidery, spaced knots and twisted threads.

If you are new to embroidered ribbon techniques, take time to practice, relax and learn the basic stitches. Then, choose your favorite project, jump into your sea of silk ribbon and begin! Some ideas require time and patience to complete, however, the majority of subjects include a "Quick Project." Avoid becoming overwhelmed. Gain confidence by beginning with a "Quick Project." When you feel comfortable, proceed to the more detailed designs. By working on a "Quick Project," you will gain new skills and/or learn new stitches.

A straight-stitch sewing machine is a requirement in the execution of ribbon embroidery by machine. On the more sophisticated techniques, such as computerized machine embroidery, we include an alternate method that requires a zigzag machine.

We hope you experience a great deal of pleasure and satisfaction in acquiring new skills!

We thank all our students, here and abroad, who have excelled in ribbon embroidery; their encouragement has prompted us to write this book.

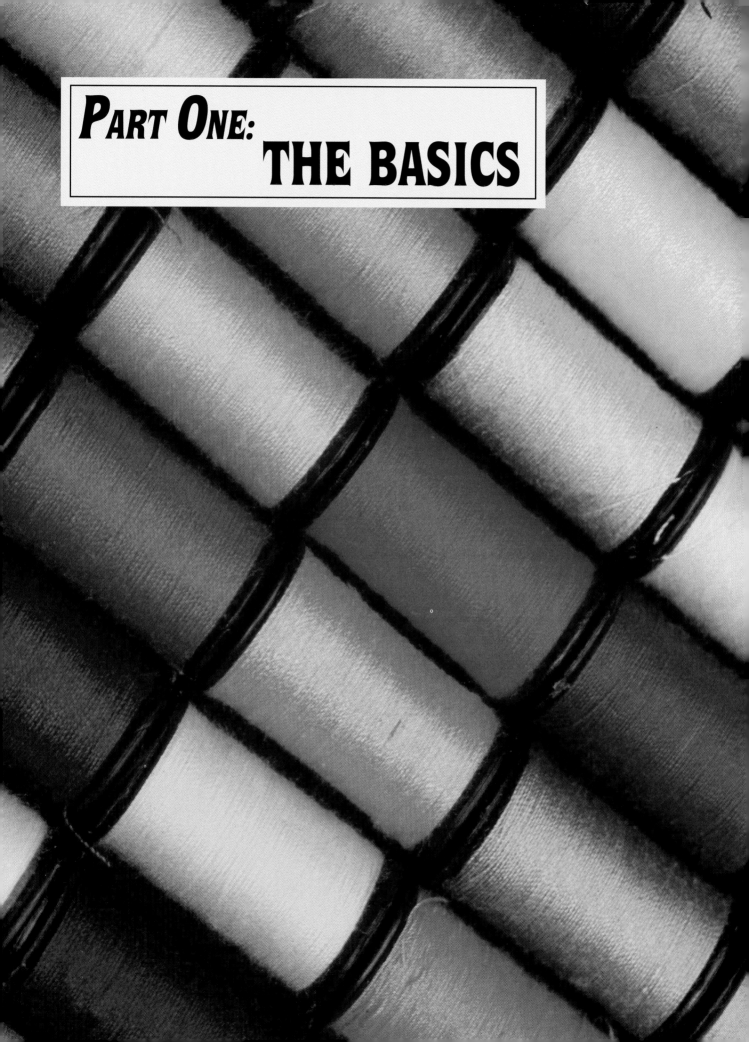

PART ONE: THE BASICS

MATERIALS AND SUPPLIES

SEWING MACHINE

A sewing machine is essential for creating ribbon embroidery by machine! Any sewing machine will work since only a straight-stitch will be used. However, a machine that allows the feed dogs to be lowered or covered is an asset. A machine with an electronic needle stop down setting is a great advantage! The more stitch by stitch control available, the better.

FABRIC

Ribbon embroidery is so versatile that it can be worked on fabric ranging from the finest silk to the heaviest denim.

The secret to success for different fabrics is gearing the type of embroidery to the type of fabric - bold designs and stitches for heavier fabrics and fine delicate patterns for the lighter weight fabrics.

HOOP

A 5" to 6" hoop is required. There are several types of hoops. The hoop must hold fabric taut and fit under the needle of the sewing machine. If working on a delicate fabric, such as silk or fine cotton, wrap the hoop with twill tape to reduce the abrasion on fabric. Spring hoops are better for knits. Take care when placing knit in the hoop or stretching will occur and distort your design.

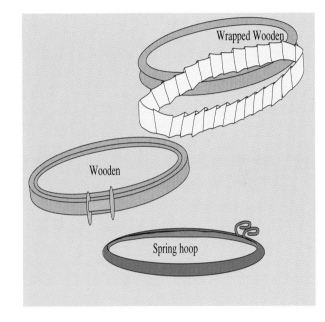

Wrapped Wooden

Wooden

Spring hoop

THREAD

Nylon or invisible thread is used in the needle and in the bobbin. YLI™, Sulky™, Coats & Clark™ and Dritz™ manufacture invisible thread in white or smoke. These are amazingly soft, and feel almost like regular thread. Invisible thread eliminates the need to change thread color. For very dark ribbons and threads, smoke colored thread is fine, however, white is translucent and virtually disappears. In most cases the ribbon will cover the thread.

Satisfactory results can be obtained by using polyester or polyester/cotton thread. The disadvantage, to using this type of thread, is the necessity to change the color thread to match the ribbon. These types of thread are much more visible than the nylon threads.

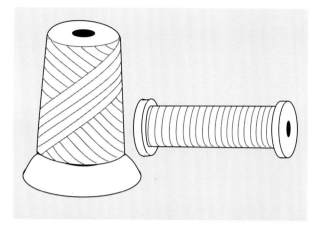

RIBBON

Embroidery ribbon is different from the decorative type of ribbon purchased at a fabric store. It is made of 100% silk or a synthetic, such as polyester or rayon. Silk embroidery ribbon is extremely soft and pliable, which allows fabulous texture to be created in flowers and foliage! The ribbon comes in 2mm, 4mm, 7mm and 13mm widths. The 4mm is the most popular and is available in approximately one hundred fifty colors.

Due to the popularity of ribbon embroidery, there are now many brands ranging in quality. Experiment with your ribbons.

Choose a colorfast ribbon if the finished item is to be washed or dry cleaned.

On bright colored silk ribbons, it is suggested that you rinse the ribbons in cold water for the first few washings.

Here is a simple test to see if the ribbon is

colorfast. Pin ribbons to a scrap of white fabric and dip them in water, gently agitate, and put in the dryer. If any color runs onto the white fabric, it is best to dry clean the finished project.

Silk ribbon can be washed or dry cleaned. Cleaning results have been good with embroidered items that have been hand and machine washed. Follow care instructions for the fabric on which you've done embroidery work. Silk ribbon can be machine dried with no need for pressing.

OPTIONAL THREADS

Occasionally we will mention different threads, such as pearl rayon. These threads are generally a heavier weight, crochet type used for detail work.

Use these threads as you do ribbon. Do not thread into the machine.

Regular embroidery floss, or crochet cotton can also be used for special effects.

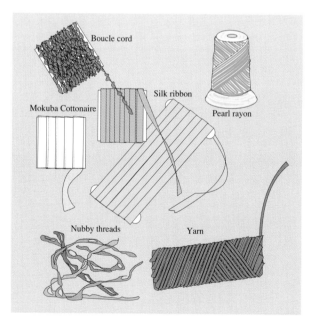

Boucle cord

Silk ribbon

Mokuba Cottonaire

Pearl rayon

Nubby threads

Yarn

NEEDLE

Always begin a project with a new needle in your sewing machine. Use a Size 80/12 Universal needle. If the needle has a burr or a rough spot, it may snag the delicate ribbon! If snagging occurs, immediately change the needle.

MARKERS

Air soluble markers are available from many manufactures. For example, Collins™, EZ-International™, and Dritz™, are available in many different colors. An air soluble marker will evaporate in 12 to 24 hours. For intricate work, use a fine line markers. Chalk pencils or tailor's chalk can be used on dark colors. Test your markers before use, especially if marks will not be completely covered by the embroidery.

TWEEZERS

Serger tweezers are used, as you sew, to hold the ribbon in place. If you have a serger, you may already have tweezers. We recommend a bent nose tweezer which is available in 5", 6" or 7" lengths. Choose the size you find most comfortable. A trolley needle can also assist in holding the ribbon in the desired position.

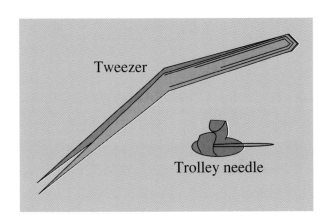

SET-UP AND TECHNIQUES

MACHINE SET-UP

Ribbon embroidery can be done on any sewing machine. Make sure the sewing machine is in good running condition. Clean the lint from the machine and oil if necessary. To begin ribbon embroidery, set up the machine for free motion work.

1. Remove the presser foot and shank. If you have snap-on feet, remove the shank attached to the presser foot by removing the screw. Consult the owners manual for details.

2. Slowly wind half a bobbin with invisible thread. Place the bobbin in the sewing machine.

3. Insert a new, size 80/12 Universal needle.

4. With the presser foot up, thread the sewing machine needle with invisible thread.

5. Drop or cover the feed dog.

(Refer to the owners manual for procedures of "sewing on a button.")

6. If the sewing machine has the option, set the needle-down feature to the down position.

7. Note the normal tension setting. Lower the top tension by one number.

8. If available on the sewing machine, engage the slow-speed feature.

9. Make a generous sewing area for the hoop by using the flat bed extension to cover the free arm.

CARE OF EMBROIDERED ITEMS

Finished ribbon embroidered items need special care. With care, the majority of ribbons can be washed and dried by machine. Turn the garment inside out, and use a gentle cycle on the washing machine. Dry at a low temperature in the dryer. Do not use high heat or over dry. The safest technique is to hand wash and hang to dry!

When dry cleaning garments, request that the garment be hand pressed to avoid flattening of ribbon embroidery.

If you are pressing the finished garments, press around the embroidery. If it is necessary to get between two designs, where the iron will not fit, use a sleeve board. Place the embroidery just off the edge, enabling you to get into little spaces! Another good way to press finished embroidery is to place it face down on a thick terry towel and gently steam. The embroidery is cushioned by the towel.

If possible, use a puff iron (smockers love them!). A puff iron is ideal for pressing "under" ribbon embroidery. It allows the fabric to be easily pressed without flattening the ribbon.

If embroidery is accidentally pressed, it can be revived with a burst of steam.

Hold the iron a few inches above the garment and press the steam button. Restore the flower shape using your fingers.

HELPFUL HINTS

Before you begin, please read these helpful hints and use as a reference. Follow these guidelines while stitching:

•Lower the presser foot lever when sewing!

•Raise the presser foot lever when threading the sewing machine! (Note that it is harder to notice the presser foot lever without a presser foot attached. Get in the habit of lowering the presser foot lever as soon as you put the hoop into the machine.)

•Work with the needle down in the fabric. If featured on the sewing machine, set the needle stop-down, or stop it in the down position.

•If the presser foot lever is not down, or the thread is not in the tension discs, a lump of threads will form underneath fabric. If this happens, re-thread the machine and lower the presser foot lever!

•If fabric bounces as you sew, or threads break frequently, fabric may not be secured tightly in the hoop.

•If threads break often, put in a new needle, or lower the sewing machine tension one more number.

•Do not worry about cutting the ribbon pieces too long. Use a container to hold the small, leftover pieces. These pieces will be convenient when you need to fill in one small space or need one color for a petal.

•Use practice projects to create ornaments or crazy patchwork pieces. Only you will know they are "scraps"!

Be patient! Keep in mind that production is always slowed when learning a new technique. The more you practice, the faster and more confident you will become at ribbon embroidery.

PART TWO:
THE STITCHES

PRELIMINARY PRACTICE with FREE MOTION STITCHING

Free motion embroidery only looks difficult. Practice the technique on a scrap of fabric. Once you have enjoyed the freedom this technique offers, you will wonder why you haven't done it sooner.

You will use free motion embroidery often, after the technique is mastered.

FREE MOTION STITCHING

Let's get started sewing!

1. Cut an 8" square of fabric and place it in the hoop. Place right side of fabric to the inside of the hoop. Place the larger ring of the hoop on a flat surface. Lay the fabric on top. Place the smaller ring on top and insert it inside the larger ring. Pull the fabric taut, and tighten the screw. If using a spring hoop, although some pulling may be necessary, tension is usually self-adjusted. If you haven't already, thread the machine and set up according to Machine Set-up instructions on page 12.

When free motion stitching, *you* are moving

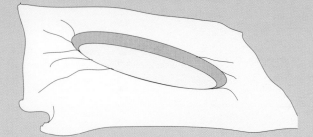

the fabric. The sewing machine is no longer feeding the fabric. This enables movement in any direction. Begin by placing the hoop under the needle, with the fabric against the bed of the machine. **Lower the presser foot!** Lowering the presser foot engages the tension, even though the presser foot has been removed from the machine. If you forget, you will get a lump of threads underneath the work!
2.

2. Draw the bobbin thread up by taking one manual stitch. Turn the fly wheel, towards you, one full turn. Draw the bobbin thread up, bringing both threads to the top of the fabric. Take three or four stitches in place and snip the thread tails. Always begin this way to keep the back neat and tidy!

Practice moving the fabric in random directions. Sew in any direction your heart desires; sideways, forward, backward, draw some circles, and practice following the lines. Keep fabric flat against the bed of the machine. **Do not lift the hoop.** After a few minutes you will be ready to start the ribbon embroidery!

BASIC STITCHES

CHAIN STITCH

The chain stitch is a commonly used embroidery stitch. It is used for roses, stems, initials and outlines. Tweezers are not needed for the chain stitch. Manipulate the ribbon with your hands.

Place fabric, right side up, in the hoop with the larger ring on the bottom. Place the hoop in the machine and put the presser foot lever down.

BASIC CHAIN STITCH

1. Holding the thread, take one stitch and pull the bobbin thread up to the surface.

Holding the threads, take a few stitches to anchor the threads. Clip the thread tails.

2. Cut a 10" to 12" length of ribbon. Take a few stitches in the center of the length of the ribbon.

3. Avoid getting the ribbon caught in stitching, hold the ribbon out of the way. Stitch forward 1/4" on the fabric.

4. Cross the ribbon in front of the needle. Adjust the tension on the ribbon. A soft fullness is desirable. Take a stitch or two across the crossed ribbons.

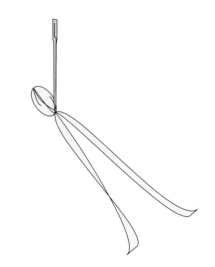

5. Keeping the ribbon out of the way, stitch 1/4". Cross the ribbon in front of the needle, and stitch. Continue repeating these steps, stitch, cross the ribbon; stitch, cross the ribbon etc.

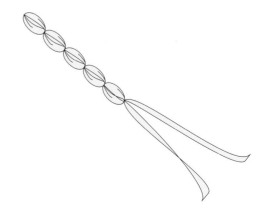

LAZY DAISY STITCH

The lazy daisy stitch, a traditional embroidery stitch, is one of the most commonly used stitches.

The projects in this book use the lazy daisy stitch for leaves, flowers, foliage and flower centers. As with all the stitches, the width of ribbon you use will determine the finished size of the lazy daisy. Experiment with 2mm, 4mm and 7mm ribbons. Keep these samples for future size reference.

A tweezers is required when working this stitch.

1. While sewing, use a tweezers to hold the ribbon in place. Use about 12" of ribbon. Anchor the end of the ribbon by taking a few stitches. Hold the ribbon out of the way, and stitch out about 1/4". Stop with the needle down.

2. Bring the ribbon around the needle and anchor with two stitches. Don't pull ribbon tight, let it lie comfortably. The ribbon should lie flat in the center and a bit pinched at the ends.

3. Hold the ribbon out of the way. Stitch back to the starting point.

4. Bring the ribbon back to the starting point and stitch to anchor. Again, don't pull ribbon tight. While sewing, shape and hold the ribbon with the tweezers.

FLAT LAZY DAISY STITCH

The flat lazy daisy stitch is similar to the lazy daisy, except, while stitching, the ribbon is kept flat. The flat lazy daisy stitch is often used to create an Iris or Tulip leaf.

1. Anchor the end of the ribbon by holding the ribbon out of the way. Stitch 1/4" to 1/2" away from the ribbon.

2. Keeping the ribbon flat, bring it over and stitch to anchor.

3. Keeping the ribbon out of the way, stitch next to the ribbon and back to the starting point.

4. Bring the ribbon around, fold it over, keep it flat, and anchor it at the starting point. Depending on the effect desired, pinch the ribbon a bit as you anchor it, but still keep the middle flat!

LAZY DAISY CHAIN

The lazy daisy chain is a running lazy daisy stitch. It is similar in looks to the chain stitch, but fuller.

1. Complete a lazy daisy stitch.

2. Stitch next to the lazy daisy, to the opposite end.

3. Bring the ribbon over and anchor.

4. Now do another lazy daisy, and repeat steps 2 and 3. Continue in this way making a chain of lazy daisies!

DOUBLE LAZY DAISY CHAIN

The lazy daisy chain stitch is an excellent choice for a crazy quilt stitch. To make it even more luxurious, try this double lazy daisy chain.

1. Use two colors of 2mm or 4mm ribbon. Make a lazy daisy chain by starting with one lazy daisy stitch.

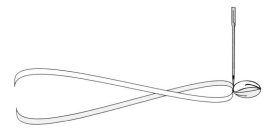

2. Stitch around the lazy daisy to the outer point.

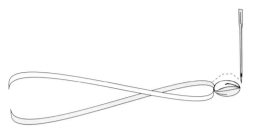

3. Bring the ribbons around, keep them flat, and anchor.

4. Continue until the desired length has been reached.

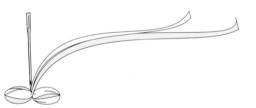

RIBBON STITCH

The ribbon stitch, or straight-stitch in hand embroidery, is  *usually done with 7mm ribbon. It gives the effect of a single stitch pulled through the fabric by holding the ribbon flat as it is stitched. For more delicate work, try working this stitch using 4mm ribbon.*

1. Start with the end of the ribbon anchored and pointed toward the area where a petal or leaf will be placed. Pinch the ribbon together and hold as you stitch.

2. Stitch 1/4" to 3/8" to the other end of the petal or leaf.

3. Fold the ribbon over so it covers the cut end. Holding the ribbon flat in the center, pinch the end and stitch over it to anchor.

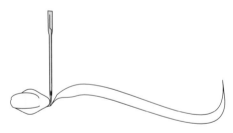

4. To finish, cut the ribbon leaving about 1/4". Tuck the end under the flower petal and stitch in place.

These petals are not connected together and are good when spaced-out stitches are desired.

RUNNING RIBBON STITCH

The running ribbon stitch is best used with 7mm and 9mm wide ribbons. This stitch is similar to the ribbon stitch, but is worked in a continuous row.

1. Start with the end of the ribbon anchored and pointed toward the area where a petal or leaf will be placed. Anchor ribbon in place.

2. Use the tweezers to hold the ribbon in place. Pinch and tack in place.

3. Stitch forward 1/4" to 1/2". Repeat step 2 to the desired length.

FERN STITCH

We named this stitch the fern stitch.

It can be used to make leaves, baskets and trellises. To our knowledge, the

fern stitch does not resemble any traditional hand stitch. It is an excellent stitch to use anytime a large area is to be filled.

1. Keeping the ribbon flat, anchor the end.

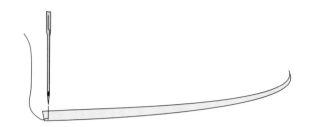

2. Hold the ribbon out of the way and stitch out 3/8".

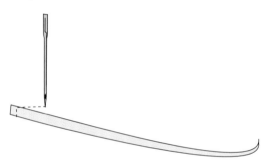

3. Keeping it flat, stitch across to anchor. Keep the ribbon out of the way and stitch back to the starting point.

4. Bring the ribbon over, keep it flat and anchor it. Envision an "accordion" while folding it back and forth.

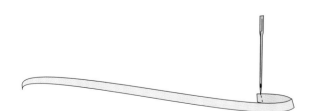

5. Continue until you have covered the desired area.

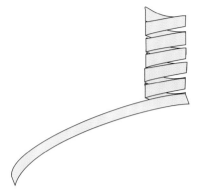

LOOSE FERN STITCH

The loose fern stitch is a variation of the traditional fern stitch which uses two ribbons simultaneously. Stitch according to the fern stitch instructions, but keep one rather taut, and allow the other to be much looser. This technique creates a nice three dimensional texture.

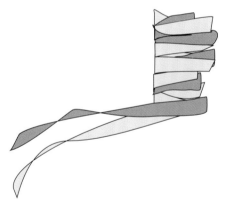

LOOPED FERN STITCH

1. Use two colors of ribbon. Tack them both at the starting position. Carry both along as explained in the fern stitch instructions.

2. Using the tweezers, create a loop to one side and tack in the center.

3. Pull a loop to the other side. Tack loop in the middle. To give the effect of "feathers" or "leaves" and create an interesting dimension, always leave one ribbon more loose than the other.

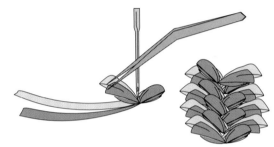

FRENCH KNOTS

French knots are easy!

1. Anchor the end of the ribbon.

With the needle down, wind the ribbon around the needle three times. Keep the ribbon tension medium, not too tight. The size of the French knot will be determined by the width of the ribbon and the number of times it is wrapped around the needle.

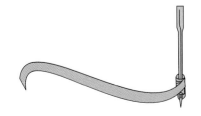

2. Holding the wrapped ribbon in place with the tweezers, stitch outside the knot to anchor. It may be more comfortable to sew this stitch by manually turning the hand wheel. French knots are often done in clusters. Try doing a couple together.

LOOSE FRENCH KNOT

A loose, more relaxed version of the traditional French knot, is the loose French knot. This stitch makes an excellent bud or portion of a flower.

1. Twist the ribbon around the needle 3-4 times, as in the French knot instructions.

2. Let the ribbon relax so it is about 1/8″ from the needle.

3. Tack in place as in the French knot instructions.

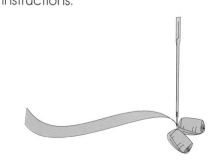

BULLION STITCH

The bullion stitch is most commonly used to make rose buds. With the exception of using 7mm ribbon and wrapping 6 times around the needle instead of 3 times, this stitch is exactly like the French knot.

1. After you have wrapped the ribbon, raise the needle by hand and move slightly to one side. Flip the "bullion" over on its side, and take a few stitches to anchor. It may help to spread the ribbon a bit, "opening" the bud before taking the anchoring stitches.

RUCHING

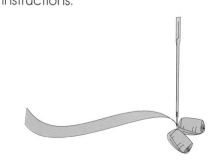

Ruching is traditionally worked by hand, gathering the ribbon down the center and then applying to fabric.

This is a gather-as-we-go technique.

1. Anchor the end of the ribbon. If you are right handed, use your left hand and hold the ribbon out to the left. If you are left-handed, reverse. With the tweezers, pull about 1/4" of ribbon to the right of the needle. Take a stitch or two to anchor. Repeat.

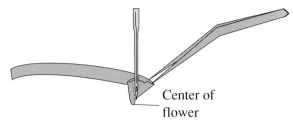

2. Continue making a row. To make a wide row, double back and make a U-turn. This technique is very effective for flowers or leaves.

SINGLE EDGED RUCHING

"Very pretty Morning Glory t y p e f l o w e r s " can be made by ruching only the edge of 7mm, 10mm or 13mm wide ribbon.

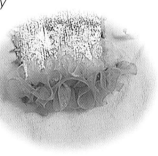

1. Always sew in the center of the flower. Begin by folding the end of the ribbon under 1/4", and anchor it flat.

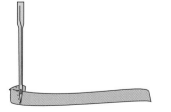

2. Using the tweezers, hold a pleat in place and stitch.

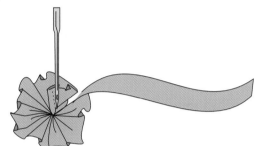

Center of flower

3. Continue, pulling another pleat and stitching. Work in a circle until the flower is complete.

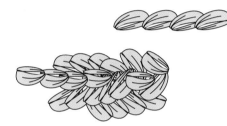

COUCHING

In some respects, all the stitches we have done can be called couching. The

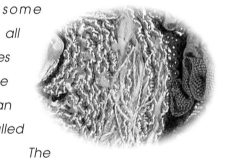

term couching means tacking a surface ribbon or thread in place, versus threading it into the sewing machine. Stems or tree branches are created by couching certain threads and ribbons.

1. Anchor the end of the ribbon by tucking it under and stitching it in place. In the case of yarns or threads, stitch over the end without tucking it under.

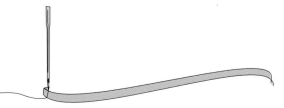

2. Sew next to the ribbon, occasionally stitching onto the ribbon to tack.

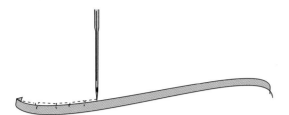

COUCHING WITH A TWIST

Couching with a twist is a nice rambling stitch, useful if working a free form or meandering design. This stitch is also very pretty on lettering and is a variation on couching.

1. Anchor the end by tucking it under, and, keeping the ribbon out of the way, stitch 1/4".

2. Twist the ribbon one half turn and anchor.

3. Continue to desired length.

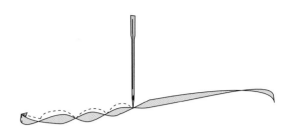

LOOP STITCH

This loop stitch is similar to ruching and will create a pretty flower.

1. Anchor at the edge of the ribbon. Hold the ribbon in your left hand, and pull a loop to the right with the tweezers. Stitch to anchor.

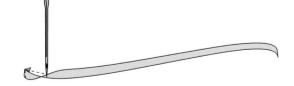

2. Continue pulling loops, making a circle. Always anchor loops in the same center spot.

LOOPED FLOWER VARIATION

A very pretty cascading type of flower, three dimensional leaves and foliage can be created by making a row of loops, instead of a circle. Follow instructions for the looped flower, working not in the center, but in a row.

FEATHER STITCH

1. Begin with two lazy daisies.

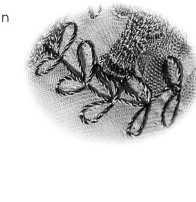

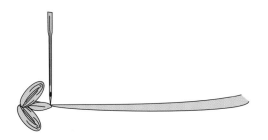

2. Stitch 1/4" and anchor the ribbon.

3. Repeat the lazy daisies from step 1, and step 2 until desired length is reached.

HALF FEATHER STITCH

The half feather stitch is similar to the regular feather stitch. Work one lazy

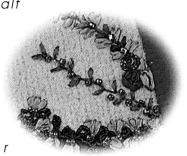

daisy stitch each time, alternating sides. Different effects can be achieved by keeping the ribbon flat, rather than scrunched.

BLANKET STITCH

1. Begin with a flat lazy daisy stitch.

2. Stitch 1/4", anchor the ribbon and repeat step 1. Continue.

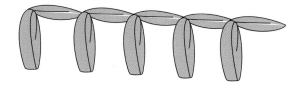

ZIGZAG STITCH

The zigzag stitch is easy!

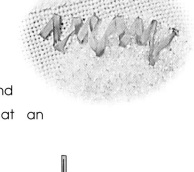

1. Anchor the end of the ribbon and stitch 1/4" at an angle.

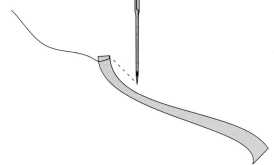

2. Keeping the ribbon flat, bring it around and anchor.

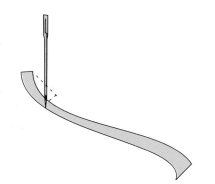

3. Stitch at an angle, fold the ribbon "accordion" style and tack it in place. This is a "stretched out" fern stitch. Repeat these steps to the desired length.

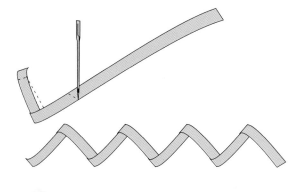

CROSS STITCH

The cross stitch is done like the zigzag stitch, but twice!

1. Start with a row of zigzag stitches. Depending on the size ribbon used, stitch rows approximately 1/2" apart. Don't stitch rows too close together.

2. Using a different color (if desired), sew back down with another row of zigzag.

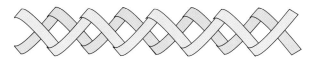

PISTOL STITCH

1. At the starting point tack down the end of the ribbon.

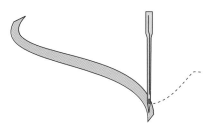

2. Keeping the ribbon flat, stitch straight up 1/4" to 1/2", bring ribbon up and stitch to anchor.

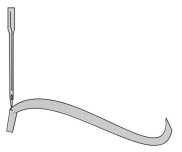

3. Make a French knot at the end and do not cut the ribbon. Stitch back to the starting point. Anchor ribbon.

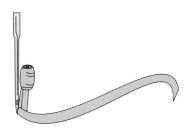

4. If desired, repeat steps 2 and 3, at a 45 degree angle.

5. For another set of pistol stitches, stitch 1/4" to 1/2" away and repeat steps 1 through 4 until desired length is completed.

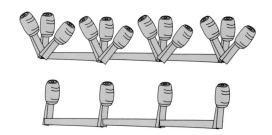

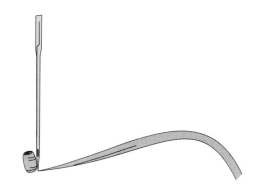

2. Stitch about 1/4" to 1/2" away and anchor the ribbon.

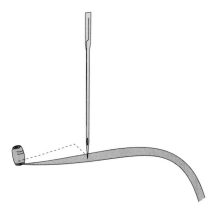

3. Make a French knot and continue steps 2 and 3 until desired length is completed.

CHAIN FRENCH KNOTS

1. Anchor 2mm or 4 m m ribbon a n d make a French knot.

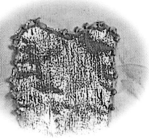

BASIC DECORATIVE EFFECTS

BASIC BEADING

Beads add glamour, highlights and fun to our ribbon embroidery! In the past you may have sewn them on by hand, but now you will learn to sew them by machine!

First things first, when purchasing beads, be sure that a THREADED sewing machine needle will fit into the bead. It is difficult to guess at the hole size, so take a threaded needle with you. Size 6/0 and 8/0 beads, by Gick™ are used in pictured projects. Any bead will work if a threaded sewing machine needle can be inserted into the bead hole. The smallest sewing

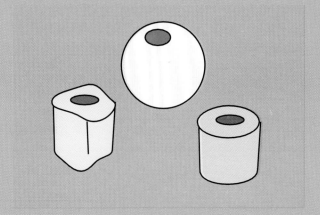

machine needle available is size 8/60.

Note: Long bugle beads (long, thin tubular beads) do not work well. Look for round or short, "square" beads as shown.

Beads are applied as the ribbon embroidery is worked. It is fast and easy to apply beads at the same time because the needle is in the right spot, and threads are securely anchored.

A student complained that most of the beads fell off her blouse when it was washed. After questioning her, we discovered that she had applied the beads *after* she was finished with the embroidery. She executed her design by starting where she wanted a bead, took two or three stitches, and put on the next bead. After two or three more stitches, she cut the threads and moved on to the next spot and started over again. This resulted in the thread coming undone because not enough stitches were sewn before and after the beads.

When you are ready to apply a bead, TAKE YOUR FOOT OFF THE FOOT CONTROL/PEDAL. Place the bead on the fabric where it is to be sewn. Manually, turn the hand wheel and insert just the tip of the needle into the bead hole.

Move the bead

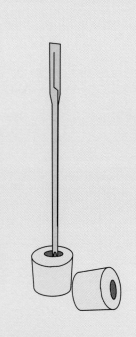

gently into position, manually turning the wheel toward you to complete a stitch. Take an additional stitch one bead width away. This will cause the bead to "pop" over on its side.

Repeat technique with additional beads.

BOBBIN THREAD EMBROIDERY

Prepare to work with decorative threads in the bobbin! This technique was used on a taupe colored linen fabric. Very attractive, decorative stitching can be done with a zigzag stitch or basic decorative stitches.

Decorative threads that are too heavy to go through the eye of a needle, work well in the bobbin. Pearl rayon, light weight yarns, metallic threads and crochet threads such as Knit Crosheen™ are wonderful in the bobbin. Because this is a tone on tone embellishment technique, match light and dark shades of thread to fabric. Wind several bobbins by hand or machine. Bypass the threading prior to the bobbin.

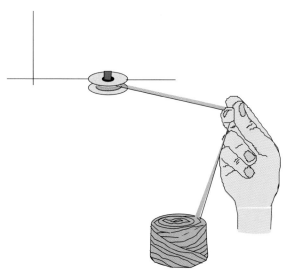

If possible, get an extra bobbin case and adjust it for heavy threads. Loosen the screw counter clockwise 1/4 turn. Place your wound bobbin in the bobbin case and pull the thread. If it feels very tight or won't pull at all, make another 1/4 turn and try again. Continue to do this until it pulls freely with a slight drag. If it is impossible to get another bobbin case, remember the required 1/4 turns and readjust case for regular sewing. Unfortunately, a built-in bobbin case may not lend itself to heavy threads. If necessary, skip this technique and move on to another exciting technique.

Prepare your fabric, and a practice scrap, by spray starching and pressing several times. Or, use one of the variety of washout fabric stiffeners on the market. If using "dry-clean only" fabrics, dry-cleaning will remove the stiffener and will usually soften as it is handled. This preparation step prevents fabric from puckering while stitching. Do not use a stabilizer, as stitching will be done with fabric right side down.

Thread matching regular thread on top and put the bobbin case into the machine. Stitch on a piece of scrap fabric. Stitching is on the bobbin side so the fabric must be **right side down** as you stitch. Try a straight-stitch, zigzag, and any open decorative stitches. Satin stitches, such as a scallop stitch, are not recommended as the heavy threads accumulate and won't feed well.

If stitches are loose, tighten tension on bobbin case by turning screw 1/4 turn clockwise. If too much top thread is showing, loosen tension on bobbin case but turning screw 1/4 turn counter clockwise.

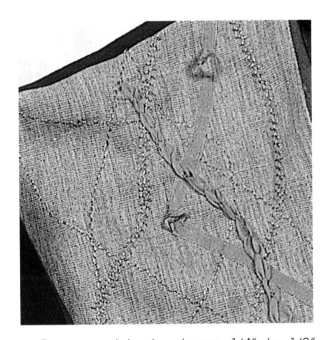

When stitches are satisfactory, begin stitching on the garment.

Leave long thread tails. End where a seam will be sewn or thread the tails onto a hand sewing needle and pull to the back side.

For spaced knots, choose 1/4" to 1/2" ribbon. An open weave, cotton ribbon by Mokuba™ was used on shirt pictured on page 00. However, a 7mm wide silk ribbon, grosgrain ribbon, satin ribbon or any kind of matching tape or ribbon is acceptable.

Set sewing machine for regular stitching. Again, begin at an edge of the fabric that will be stitched into a side or shoulder seam. Straight-stitch 1 - 2" on the edge of the ribbon. Stop and tie an overhand knot. Lift the presser foot and "jump" over the knot. Continue to straight-stitch on the edge for another 3 or 4 inches.

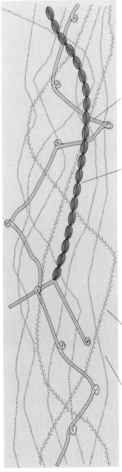

Spaced knots sewn with 7mm to 9mm ribbon

Chain stitch sewn with 7mm to 9mm ribbon

Decorative threads such as pearl rayon in the bobbin: Feather stitch

Straight stitch

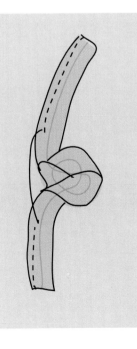

Randomly sew and occasionally turn a corner by folding the ribbon.

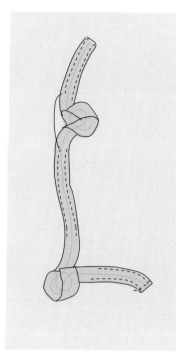

End in a seam or turn the end of the ribbon 1/4" under. Stitch in place. Stitch down the other side of the ribbon.

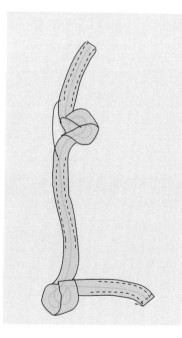

CREATING TWISTED THREAD

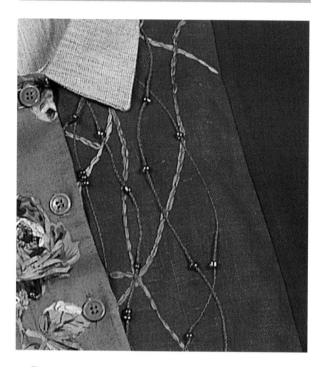

The twisted thread technique can be accomplished on any sewing machine with an external bobbin winder.

Choose pearl rayon, two strands of a fine yarn, or multiple strands (four to six) of a sewing weight thread. Measure out two yards of each thread. Depending on the thickness of the thread, two and six threads will be used. A yarn does not need as many strands as a silk floss. The weight of the fabric should determine how heavy to make the cords. Place the thread ends in the large center hole of the bobbin.

Place the bobbin on the bobbin winder, and

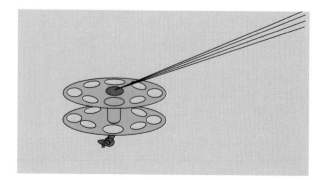

hold the thread ends straight up and out.

With threads held tightly in your hand, hold the thread ends taut and run the bobbin winder. This will twist the threads. Continue running the machine until you feel your hand pulling in towards the machine. Stop the machine, but continue to hold the twisted threads taut. Using your other hand, hold the thread half way down, and fold it in half. **Hold**

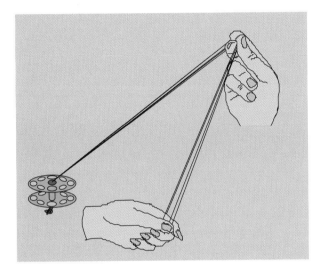

taut at all times. Release the folded end, and continue to hold the loose ends together. Remove the bobbin from the bobbin winder. It is normal for threads to be tangled. Holding the loose ends, run the threads between your fingers and straighten them out. The result will be a cord, where the threads have twisted back on themselves. Tie a knot at the loose ends.

Thread seven or eight beads into the twisted cord. Place the knotted end in an area where a seam will be sewn. Thread machine with a matching thread. Set sewing machine for a narrow zigzag, with a 2 width and 2 length. Slide the beads to the middle of the cord. Zigzag over the cord. Curve randomly for several inches. Lift the presser foot and slide one bead

in place. "Jump" over the bead and continue stitching another four or five inches. Repeat to the end of the cord. This is considered a "good end" and it is not necessary to hide in a seam. If desired, create several more cords. See diagram for cord placement.

Add a chain stitch, randomly interspersed with silk ribbon to match the fabric.

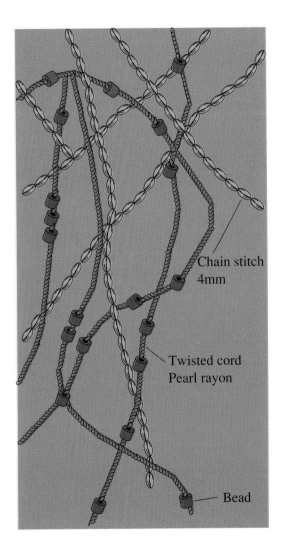

Chain stitch 4mm

Twisted cord Pearl rayon

Bead

PART THREE:
THE PROJECTS

APPLIQUÉ FISH T-SHIRT

Appliqué is a wonderful way to bring color and design into your work.

Designs are not limited to fish, try embellishing flowers or any motif you like!

T-shirt, tote bag, dress, jumper, jean jacket or vest
Cotton print fabric with motif
Beads: multicolored pastel beads size 8/0, opalescent size 6/0
Threads: purple boucle cord, blue-green pearl rayon, coordinating rayon embroidery thread, white or black bobbin thread, (fine) size 60
Tear-away stabilizer

Appliqué is quick, easy and fun! Choose a large print fabric with a 2″ to 5″ motif. Cut out motif and appliqué. Make stitching easier by choosing shapes with smooth, simple lines. Pictured model shows appliquéd fish on a T-shirt. Designs are also wonderful on a tote bag, a dress, a jumper, a jean jacket or a vest!

To prevent fabric "bleed," always pre-wash appliqué fabric. If washable, pre-wash garment to be appliquéd. Try on the garment and mark off appliqué areas with chalk or an air soluble marker.

Choose one of the following appliqué methods. Method one is suggested for soft fabrics such as a T-shirt. Although methods refer to "fish," instructions apply to all motifs.

APPLIQUÉ METHOD ONE

Cut 1/4″ to 1/2″ around fish motif.

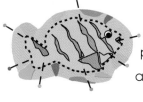

Pin fish in place. Straight-stitch around edge.

Trim to the stitching line, using an appliqué scissors or small sharp embroidery scissors.

APPLIQUÉ METHOD TWO

This is a speed method of appliqué.

Following manufacturer instructions, apply Wonder-Under™© or a similar fusible web product to the back of your fish fabric, cut the fish and tear off paper backing.

Place fish on garment and use an iron to fuse in place. Stiffness may result in the fusing process.

APPLIQUÉ

Set the sewing machine to a zigzag stitch with a width of 3 and a length of .05 or "fine." Stitches should lay close together, touching with no overlaps. Use an appliqué or satin stitch foot, which has a tunnel cut underneath, allowing stitches with bulk to feed smoothly. The length is too short if stitches accumulate and catch. Using tear away stabilizer, test stitches on a scrap piece of fabric.

You are ready to appliqué! Place a square of tear away stabilizer on the underside of the garment, under a fish. Cover the raw edge by stitching around the fish. Repeat with remaining fish then tear off stabilizer.

Add some seaweed and coral. Following the set-up instructions on page 12, set the machine for ribbon embroidery. Begin stitching seaweed an inch or two below the fish. With blue-green pearl rayon use a feather or half feather stitch. As you near the mouth of a fish, stitch over it and add some bead bubbles to appear as though they are coming from the mouth. Space beads 1/4″ to 1/2″ apart.

After completing seaweed, return to the bottom and couch some coral with purple boucle thread.

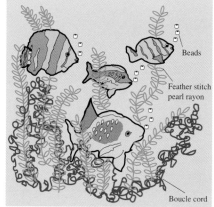

Beads

Feather stitch pearl rayon

Boucle cord

QUICK PROJECT
FISH TOWELS

Try the techniques on a set of hand towels using one fish, some seaweed and bubbles!

Because the pearl rayon tends to get buried, it is not easily visible on terry towel. Use a luxurious satin rat-tail cord. This type of cord is 1/8" wide and "satin" in appearance. A 4mm ribbon or any 1/8" cording is acceptable. Try satin rat-tail cord on a heavier garment like a sweater or sweatshirt.

MATERIALS

Two hand towels
Cotton print with fish motif - 1/3 yard
Threads: purple boucle cord
Ribbon: green rat tail cord - 3 yards or 4mm ribbon
Beads: multicolored size 8/0, opalescent size 6/0

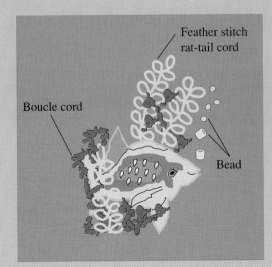

Feather stitch rat-tail cord

Boucle cord

Bead

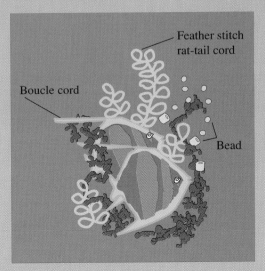

Feather stitch rat-tail cord

Boucle cord

Bead

MACHINE EMBROIDERED FISH ON DENIM SHIRT

Silk ribbon embroidery can be worked on a denim shirt, a T-shirt, a sweatshirt, a jacket or a vest. The shirt need not be ready-made, it can be a work in progress!

MATERIALS

Purchased denim shirt (shown), T-shirt, sweatshirt, jacket or vest
Sewing machine with computerized embroidery capabilities
(alternative : stencil the fish)
Threads: rayon embroidery threads in assorted pastel colors for fish embroidery, pearl rayon, sea green and white boucle thread
Ribbon: 9mm light green Cottonaire© by Mokuba™
Beads: opalescent size 6/0, multicolored pastel size 8/0

This project requires free-hand embroidery skills, or a sewing machine with hoop embroidery capabilities.

For free-hand embroidery, use coloring books or appliqué patterns as a guideline to creating your own fish! Another option is to stencil fish designs! If you prefer appliqué, see the project on page 35 for instructions using "fish" cut from printed fabric.

Mark design area. Pockets can be removed from a ready made shirt, allowing any resulting lines to dictate the design area perimeters.

Stencil or embroider fish to shirt. If necessary, follow sewing machine instructions.

Embellish with coral, seaweed and bubbles! Begin with coral at the bottom using white boucle cord by Mokuba™ and couch it in place.

Beginning at the bottom, sew seaweed with 9mm wide ribbon such as Cottonaire© by Mokuba™. Use the half feather stitch and the single chain stitch. Create more seaweed by using the feather stitch with pearl rayon. Let the stitches "meander" around or over the fish. Create the illusion of seaweed behind the fish by stopping stitch at one edge of the fish and beginning again on the other edge of the fish.

If coming near the mouth of the fish while stitching the seaweed, stitch over and sew some bead "bubbles". Beading instructions are on page 29. Use a large bead near mouth and stitch upward with progressively smaller beads.

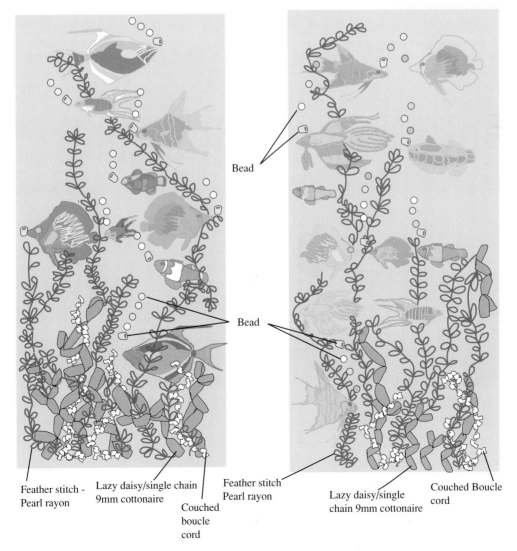

Bead

Bead

Feather stitch - Pearl rayon

Lazy daisy/single chain 9mm cottonaire

Couched boucle cord

Feather stitch Pearl rayon

Lazy daisy/single chain 9mm cottonaire

Couched Boucle cord

QUICK PROJECT
EYEGLASS CASE

This is an excellent project to try new techniques.

MATERIALS

Woven fabric, denim, cotton, linen, linen blend, velvet or satin for outer case - 1/3 yard

Cotton or polyester for lining - two 5" x 8" pieces

Fleece or batting - two 5" x 8" pieces

Ribbon: 9mm wide pale green Cottonaire© by Mokuba™

Threads: white boucle for coral, seagreen pearl rayon

Beads: pastel colors for bubbles

right sides together. Stitch two long sides and bottom edge, this time leave a 4" opening on one side. This opening will be used to turn the project right side out.

Right sides together, place the lining inside outer case and stitch across the top. Turn right side out and near the edges, use a straight-stitch to close the opening.

Draw a 5" x 8" rectangle on woven fabric. Leave enough fabric outside the rectangle to fit in a hoop. Stitch one or two fish.

Set sewing machine for ribbon embroidery, see page 12. Begin with the 9mm Cottonaire© and stitch seaweed using the half feather stitch. Additional seaweed can be created with pearl rayon using the feather stitch. Finish embroidery by adding some "bubbles" with beads and "coral" with couched boucle thread.

Finish eyeglass case by trimming the embroidered rectangle to 5" x 8". Place one piece of batting on the wrong side of the fabric and zigzag the edges together. Repeat for the other 5"x8" piece. Place embroidered rectangle and plain rectangle, right sides together.

Stitch two long sides and bottom edge to form the eyeglass case. Place two lining pieces

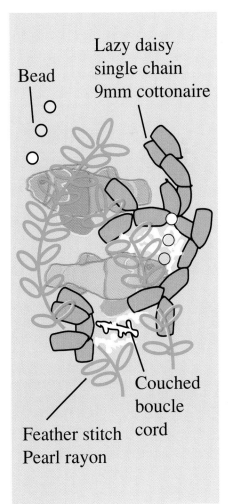

Bead

Lazy daisy single chain 9mm cottonaire

Feather stitch Pearl rayon

Couched boucle cord

CHILDREN'S MOTIFS

Children appreciate having their clothes enhanced, especially if the theme pertains to one of their favorite interests.

We have chosen to do a ballet motif for girls, using appliqué techniques with the silk ribbon embroidered embellishments.

This is a good beginner or quick project.

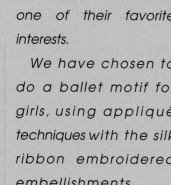

BALLERINA MOTIF ON T-SHIRT DRESS

MATERIALS

Silver lame - 1/8 yard
Silk ribbon: pink in 2mm and 4mm
Chiffon ribbon: 13mm - light pink and dark pink
Ultrasuede™ or washable felt - 4" scraps of light green
White T-shirt dress with bottom ruffle
Fusible web

Trace ballerina dress and ballet shoes onto lame. Follow manufacturer instructions and back lame with fusible web. Trace suitcase design onto Ultrasuede™© or felt. Back with fusible web. Cut on traced lines.

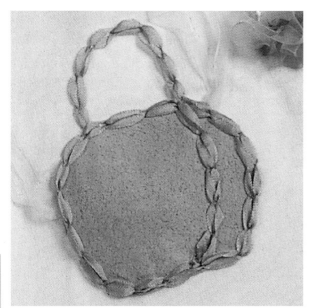

On T-shirt dress, do a freeform design. Follow the general layout guidelines. Make the couching with a twist stitch using 13mm chiffon ribbon. Position the lame dress bodice, shoes and suitcase and iron into position. Form the

skirt of the ballerina dress, using the single edge ruching stitch. Tack the top of the ribbon 3/8" below the bottom edge of the bodice (bottom ruffle will be sewn first). Fold the ends under and stitch in place. Repeat for the upper ruffle and attach it to the bottom edge of the bodice.

Stitch chained French knots around the bodice. Using 4mm pink ribbon, stitch a chain stitch to outline the suitcase and shoes. Finally, couch 4mm pink ribbon for the "ties" of the ballet shoes.

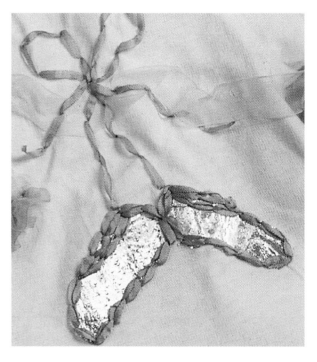

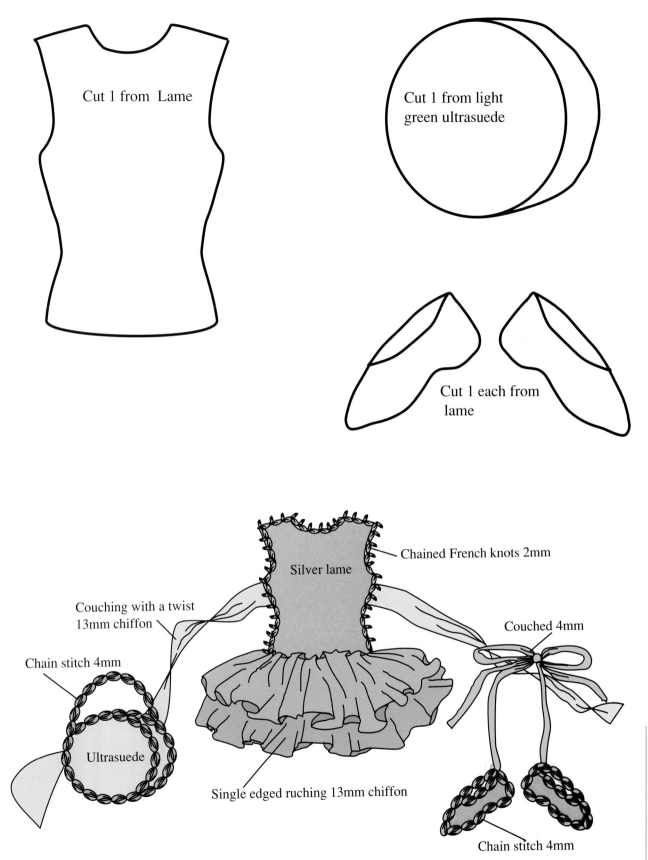

Cut 1 from Lame

Cut 1 from light green ultrasuede

Cut 1 each from lame

Chain stitch 4mm

Couching with a twist 13mm chiffon

Chained French knots 2mm

Silver lame

Couched 4mm

Ultrasuede

Single edged ruching 13mm chiffon

Chain stitch 4mm

TRAIN DESIGN

where the golden spike was driven, joining
West coast. **Follow the dots** to see what
first cross-country train looked like.

MATERIALS

Sweatshirt
Silk ribbon: 2mm - black,
        7mm - over-dyed red,
        yellow, blue and brown
Thread: green boucle cord
Beads: multicolored
Buttons: eight 3/8" multicolored

Boys seem to go through a stage (2 to 4 years old) during which they are all consumed by trains!

It is the first thing he spots in a book, at a store or off the roadside. Each train he sees is as big a thrill as the last one. Create a train for him to wear on his chest. This tells the world of his passion of the moment.

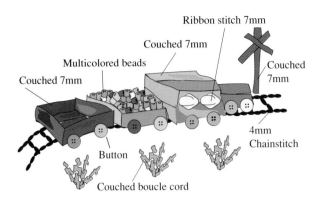

Couched 7mm
Multicolored beads
Couched 7mm
Ribbon stitch 7mm
Couched 7mm
Couched 7mm
4mm Chainstitch
Button
Couched boucle cord

Sketch the outline of the train, tracks, bushes and crossing. Begin by stitching the tracks with a chainstitch using 2mm black ribbon. The tracks do not need to go under the train cars. Start and stop as necessary. Using the 7mm ribbon as indicated, couch in place to form the train cars. As you work, tuck under the ends of the ribbon. Perspective is important on this project. Work the "back" stitches first, which will be covered by the side and front stitches. Study the "caboose."

The first ribbon is in the furthest side.

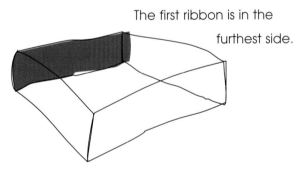

The second is the floor.

The third is the front.

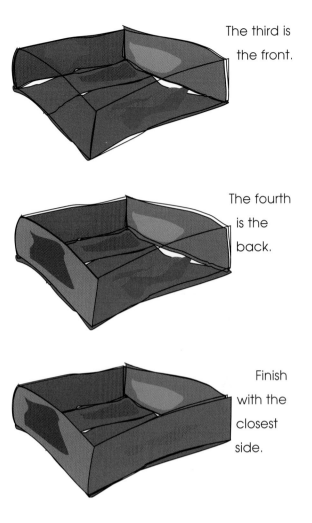

The fourth is the back.

Finish with the closest side.

Follow this technique to create the remaining cars.

Add the bushes, by couching the boucle cord. Add the crossing with brown 7mm ribbon. Embellish with the button wheels and beaded "coal." Create windows with the ribbon stitch.

COLOR BLOCKING

Color blocking is a method of combining, within the same garment, different colors, fabrics and textures in large sections. The pictured shirt is a combination of 100% linen, a linen/rayon blend and various rayon fabrics. Fabric selection started with the taupe rayon rose print. Selected coordinating solids were based around this rose print fabric. The embellishment on the rose is done with ribbon embroidery by machine. Several other ribbon techniques are used in various sections. Some techniques include beads! This project is also suitable as a jacket or a vest.

EMBELLISHED COLOR BLOCKED BLOUSE

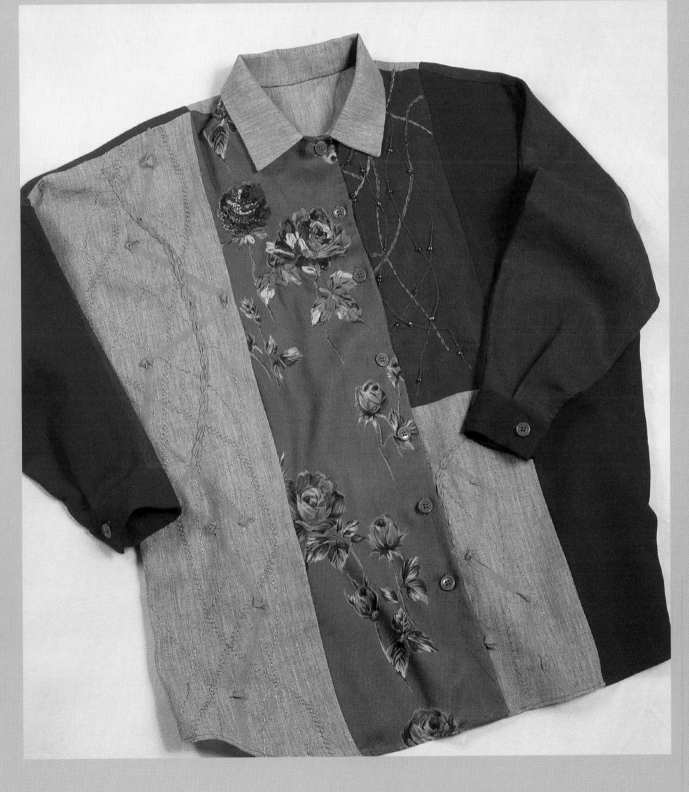

Commercial pattern for shirt, jacket or vest

One large print fabric

Assorted coordinating solids or small prints*

Assorted ribbons and beads to coordinate with fabric, choose some 2mm, 4mm, 7mm and 9mm-10mm

Threads: pearl rayon or crochet thread for twisted cord with beads - topstitching thread or pearl rayon for bobbin work, sewing weight thread in coordinating colors

Beads: assorted sizes and colors to coordinate with fabrics

Large hand sewing needle

Spray starch of fabric stiffener

*small areas such as collars, cuffs and small blocks may require 1/4 yard, however most pieces will require 1/2 yard or 1 full yard.

Choose a focal point fabric, such as the pictured rose print. When this fabric was purchased, it was simply one of those items that jumped off the rack exclaiming, "Buy me!" The fabric was irresistible! The more we pondered the uses of this fabric, the more it said "Embellish me!" This fabric originally was made into a long, flowing skirt! However, an embellished skirt draws attention to areas of our bodies that are not necessarily attractive! We decided to cut the skirt apart into a pair of long loose shorts and use the remaining fabric as part of a color blocked shirt!

When embellishing fabric with a print, choose fairly large flowers or motifs. A small all over print will not lend itself well to embellishment. The pictured fabric lends itself better to a shirt, than to a jacket or vest, because it is a light weight, rayon fabric which is flowing in nature. If you are making a jacket or vest, use a stable fabric, or back a light weight fabric with fusible interfacing.

While choosing a pattern, decide on the type of garment you would like to design. Choose a simple pattern with no darts or gathers. The most desirable patterns for color blocking are those with seams or yokes that easily break up the garment. Jacket and vest patterns are best lined to cover color blocking seams.

Study the total yardage requirements. Sit down with a paper and pencil and sketch or trace the garment. Mark the existing seams then try different possibilities for color blocking. Study diagrams for possibilities. Sections should be fairly large. The front should be broken into no more than five to seven areas and no less than two or three areas.

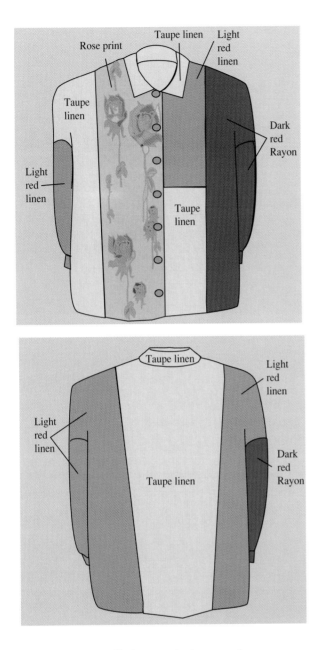

By doing preliminary design work, you can better determine yardage to be purchased. Study the pattern pieces and, in pencil, mark possible breaks. This allows you to measure the lengths and widths of the various pieces. At this point, DO NOT cut anything apart, as lengths and widths may change after fabrics have been chosen. In the pictured project, sufficient length required miscellaneous 1/2 yard cuts and one or two full yard pieces. This allowed the selected color to run the full length of the garment.

Keep in mind, vertical lines are typically more flattering than horizontal lines. Try to use several side by side, full length sections, rather than two or three short sections one on top of the other.

The rayon print used in the pictured project is dry clean only, so there was no concern about how well the coordinating fabrics washed. If dry cleaning is not preferred, be sure all the fabrics you choose are washable. Pre-wash all machine washable fabrics.

Choose fabrics of the same shade, color or quality of color. An easy way to check fabric combinations is to stand back, squint eyes and study fabric. All fabrics should blend with no one color dominating. The basic colors in the pictured shirt are taupe and red. Taupe ranges from dark, in the background of the rose print, to a lighter linen blend. The reds are all muted, dusty shades ranging from pale mauves, in the roses, to darker reds in the linen and linen blend solids. In addition to shades, also experiment with textures.

After fabric is chosen, study sketched diagrams for placement, evaluate where each fabric will be placed and prepare to cut!

To draw attention, the main focal fabric should be placed near your face. Note that only the top half of the rose fabric has been embellished, even though it extends the full length of the blouse. Only the front of this blouse has been embellished. The back of the blouse also lends itself to embellishment. Be aware that beads and knots are rather uncomfortable to sit on and lean against!

Mark a cutting line on the pattern piece. Cut apart the pattern pieces and add seam allowance. Add seam allowance by taping on another piece of paper to pattern piece or add them as you cut from fabric. If serging pieces together, use a 1/4" seam allowance. If seams are to be pressed open, use a 5/8" seam allowance. If you prefer not to cut the pattern pieces, trace them off onto tracing paper or pattern making material.

While placing pattern pieces onto the print fabric, try to visualize the areas to be embellished with ribbon embroidery. Position the pieces over "flowers" in such a way as to not cut the motif in half! It is helpful to trace the pattern onto the fabric before cutting. Remove the pattern piece and check for proper position.

Cut pieces from fabric and sew together the areas cut apart. For example, if the left front was cut into three sections, assemble them to form an entire left front. If garment will not be lined, finish seam edges with a serger or use a sewing machine on a zigzag or overlock stitch.

At this point begin the embellishment. It is easier to work on a single piece than a finished garment. Ribbon ends can be hidden in the side and shoulder seams.

Study the print fabric and decide which areas to embellish. Remember to keep the focus near the top half of the garment and choose coordinating ribbons. New designs will not be created on this garment. Texture and shading will be added to the existing fabric design.

Set sewing machine for ribbon embroidery, page 12, and place fabric in a hoop. We used a combination of the chain stitch, page 16, and lazy daisy stitch, page 17. Following the printed design, stitch ribbon over the flower, and work in from the outside. Don't cover the whole design. Simply outline the different areas

and enhance the existing colors. While working into the center, stop occasionally and

randomly add a bead. See page 29 for beading instructions.

Twisted thread was created on light red linen and strung beads were added.

The bobbin thread, page 30, and twisted

thread techniques, page 32, were used on the remaining section of the shirt.

Next, choose 1/4" to 1/2" ribbon for spaced knots. An open weave, cotton ribbon by Mokuba™ was used on pictured shirt. However,

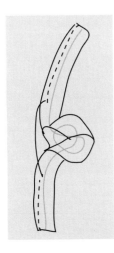

a 7mm wide silk ribbon, grosgrain ribbon, satin ribbon or any kind of matching tape or ribbon is acceptable.

Set sewing machine for regular stitching. Again, begin at an edge of the fabric that will be stitched into a side or shoulder seam. Straight-stitch 1" - 2" on the edge of the ribbon. Stop and tie an overhand knot. Lift the presser foot and "jump" over the knot. Continue to straight-stitch on the edge for another 3 or 4 inches.

Randomly sew and occasionally turn a corner by folding the ribbon.

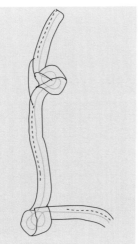

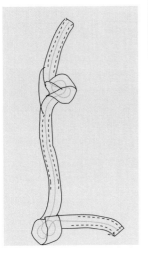

End in a seam or turn the end of the ribbon 1/4" under. Stitch in place. Stitch down the other side of the ribbon.

This section finishes with the chain stitch. Set your machine for regular straight-stitching. Thread with a matching thread. Choose silk or woven cotton ribbon such as a 3/8", loosely woven Mokuba™ ribbon.

Stitch over the center of the ribbon to anchor. Stop with the needle down, raise the presser foot and place the ends of the ribbon on top of the foot.

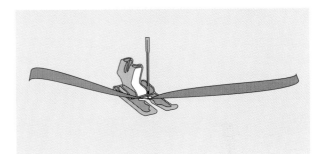

Take three stitches and stop with the needle in a down position. Cross the ribbon in front of the needle, hold the ends to the side, and take three more stitches.

Continue in this manner, creating random curves. To finish, tuck the ends under 1/4" and stitch in place, or position end at an edge that will be seamed or hemmed.

Construct your garment according to pattern directions. If beads or knots are too close to a seam line, try using a zipper foot to stitch close to them.

QUICK PROJECT COLOR BLOCKED PURSE

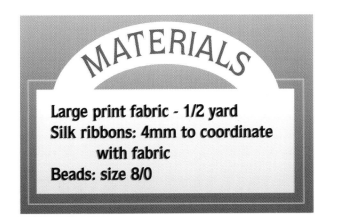

Large print fabric - 1/2 yard
Silk ribbons: 4mm to coordinate
with fabric
Beads: size 8/0

With this project, try the ribbon embellishment and beading technique shown on the rose fabric.

Mark 10" x 11" section for the bag front. "Center" the motif on the fabric. Cut another piece 10" x 11" for the back of the bag. Cut three 1" x 20" pieces. Following the directions on page 00, stitch your ribbon embroidery and beads on the bag front.

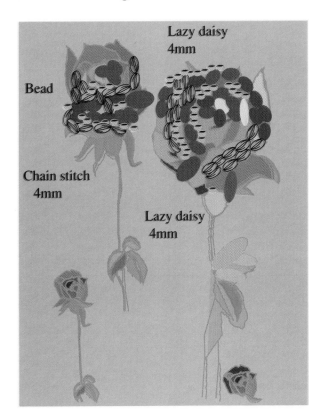

Bead

Lazy daisy
4mm

Chain stitch
4mm

Lazy daisy
4mm

Place bag front and bag back right sides together. Stitch one side seam. Right sides together, stitch one 20" strip across the top.

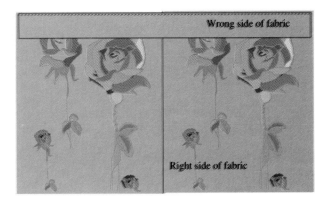

Wrong side of fabric

Right side of fabric

Form the casing for the drawstring by pressing the top raw edge under 1/4" and stitch.

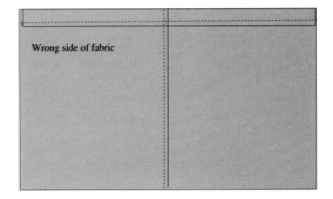

Wrong side of fabric

Leaving a space at the top for the drawstring to come out of the casing, fold right sides together and stitch the bottom and remaining side.

To make the drawstring, stitch the two remaining strips of fabric together to form one long strip. Fold under each long edge and press. Fold in half and stitch the length.

Fasten a safety pin on one end and thread through the casing. Tie a knot on each end.

BIRDS

This project is a very special gift for the bird lover in your life. It can also be a wonderful addition to a "focus wall."

This framed work of art will definitely attract attention!

The quick project is a pillow, which can feature your favorite bird square.

"IT'S FOR THE BIRDS!"

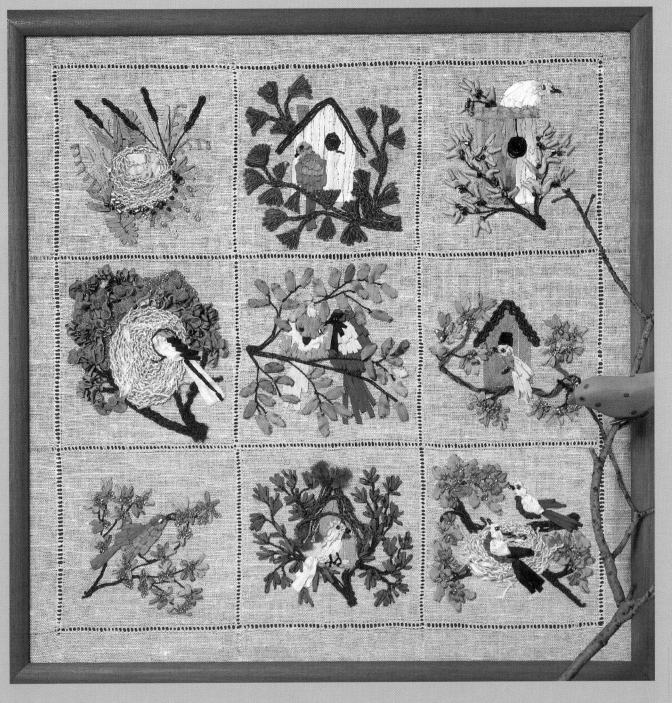

A true Irish linen was used in the pictured project. Nothing compares to the touch and appearance of true Irish linen! The threads in Irish linen stay in place after hemstitching is complete.

Any textured cotton-linen blend or similar fabric in your favorite color will work great! Avoid knits or fabrics with high polyester contents as these fabrics do not hemstitch well.

MATERIALS

54"-60" linen or linen/cotton blend,
taupe/natural color - 2/3 yard
Cotton or lining fabric - 22" square
of a dark color
Thread: matching 50 or 60 weight,
matching regular sewing
thread
Wing needle - size 100 or 120
Ribbons, Threads, Cording:

Square 1
maroon boucle cord; dark
brown pearl rayon; silk
ribbon: 2mm - medium green,
4mm - medium green,
brownish-green, yellow-green;
7mm - light blue; 9mm -
Cottonaire© tan

Square 2
dark brown yarn; dark green
yarn; dark brown pearl rayon;
silk ribbon: 4mm - mauve,
coral; 7mm - over-dyed
cream; 9mm - Cottonaire©
olive green

Square 3
dark brown yarn; brown pearl
rayon; silk ribbon: 4mm -
white, cream; 7mm - over-
dyed brown tones/cream,
over-dyed yellow-green

Square 4
reddish brown yarn; taupe
boucle cord; "nubby" cotton
yarn in beige tones; silk
ribbon: 4mm - black, mauve;
7mm - mauve, over-dyed dark
green, over-dyed cream; 9mm
- Cottonaire© gold

Square 5
dark brown pearl rayon; silk
ribbon: 4mm - taupe, cream,
medium brown, black; 7mm -
over-dyed dark green

Square 6
dark red boucle cord; medium
brown yarn; dark brown pearl
rayon; silk ribbon: 4mm -
medium green, yellow green,
brownish green, cream, coral,
black; 9mm - Cottonaire©
olive green

Square 7
dark brown pearl rayon; silk
ribbon: 4mm - yellow green,
brownish green, mauve, coral

Square 8
medium brown yarn; pearl
rayon - black, cream; silk
ribbon: 2mm - dark green;
4mm - cream, white; 9mm -
Cottonaire© white, taupe

Square 9
taupe boucle cord; nubby
cotton yarn in beige tones;
dark brown yarn; 4mm -
mauve, coral, dark purple,
black, dark red, dark brown,
dark pink; 7mm - medium
green; 9mm - Cottonaire©
white

Beads: eyes and details - dark brown
size 6/0 berries - 6/0 clear and
8/0 pink tones
Stretcher Bars -18"
Square Frame - 18"
Open Toe Appliqué Foot (optional)

FABRIC PREPARATION

Cut a 24" square, which is enough fabric to hoop and stretch around stretcher bars. Fold square in quarters and finger press to find the center. Measuring from the center, pull threads to mark a 16" square.

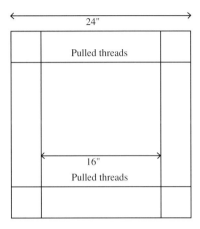

Threads are pulled to assure that fabric is straight and on grain. While hemstitching, the pulled threads will be part of the stitching procedure. After marking the 16" square, divide into 9 equal segments, which will be approximately 5 1/4" squares. Again, pull threads. Depending on the weave of the linen, remove 3 to 5 threads from each line. The removal of threads creates a 1/8" open area called an empty area. Experiment and perfect hemstitching by pulling threads on a scrap. The scrap needs to be the same fabric and can be the extra edge of the large square.

	5 1/4" square	5 1/4" square	5 1/4" square	
	5 1/4" square	5 1/4" square	5 1/4" square	
	5 1/4" square	5 1/4" square	5 1/4" square	

Hemstitching was originally done by hand. Hemstitching machines were invented in the early 19th century. Hemstitching services were available, to the general public, through local dry cleaners or department stores. Hemstitching was charged by the inch.

Our friend Sue Hausmann, a "machine person", came across one and brought it home. Because the machine was so heavy, it was thought that her floor needed structural reinforcement. The machine definitely had "power draw" when she operated it! It was similar to a "Mac Truck" with 4 needles and 2 needles and a "fabric spreader"! Fortunately, today, hemstitching can be done on almost any sewing machine! So, let's do it!

Use pulled threads as guide lines. Thread machine with 50 or 60 weight matching thread on top and in the bobbin. Using a wing needle, sew one of the following stitches, depending on machine capabilities.

"Stretch" or "reverse action" stitches are ideal for hemstitching. These stitches take two stitches forward and one stitch back. If the following stitches are not available, use a regular zigzag stitch.

Straight Stretch Stitch
Rick Rack or Stretch Zigzag
Blanket Stitch
Entredeaux

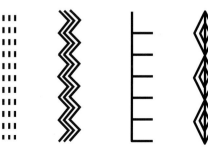

Sew one row of stitching, go in and out of the "empty threads" created by pulled threads.

Pivot and go back up the row, the needle should go into the same holes. An "open toe appliqué foot" helps guide direction.

Continue until all lines are finished. The "canvas" is now prepared for embroidery!

Set the sewing machine for ribbon embroidery. See page 12 for instructions.

Note diagram for square number identification and location. Each square has a corresponding full size diagram. Specific directions are included in order of stitching.

If desired, substitute ribbon types or colors. There are hundreds of suitable possibilities! Follow the general guidelines. If a project calls for boucle cord by Mokuba™, and this is not available, use any bumpy thread. Colors are only suggestions. Diagrams refer to the millimeter size of the silk ribbons, or the type of thread such as boucle cord. See page 15 - 27 for referenced stitches. Details on specific flowers are found in "Ribbon Embroidery by Machine" by Marie Duncan and Betty Farrell, published by Chilton; a division of Krause Publications in October, 1996.

1.	2.	3.
4.	5.	6.
7.	8.	9.

Square 1

Sketch the shape of the nest. Couch the boucle cord and nubby cotton yarns, leaving random loose tails. Add the fern, the other greenery and the cat-tails. Using the ribbon stitch, add eggs. Finish with beads.

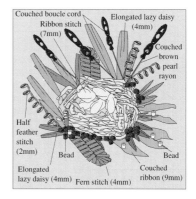

Square 2

Sketch the bird house shape. Using 7mm ribbon, couch in place to make the bird house. The entry hole is pearl rayon couched in a circle. Couch the roof, using pearl rayon. Add the chimney by couching 9mm Cottonaire© ribbon. Draw a rough outline of the tree branch. Stitch the bird before working branch. Couch the brown yarn in place for the tree branch. Use green yarn to form pine fronds. Couch the yarn in place.

Square 3

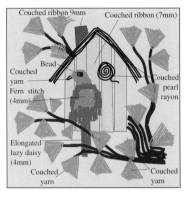

Make the outline of the bird house. Couch 7mm ribbon in place. The entry hole is pearl rayon couched in a circle. Add the bird using 4mm ribbon and the fern stitch. Draw a rough outline of the branches and couch dark brown ribbon in place. Finish with the bouillon leaves and beads.

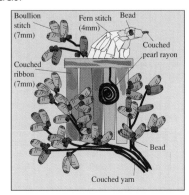

Square 4

Sketch the outline of the nest. Leaving a hole for the entry, couch boucle cord and nubby cotton yarn in place. Start on the outside of the circle and work in. Draw a rough outline of the branches and couch yarn in place. Sew bird in place. Use 7mm cream and 4mm black ribbon to create a tail, using the elongated lazy daisy stitch. Couch 7mm cream ribbon for the lower body of the bird. Create the upper body using the fern stitch with 4mm black ribbon. Couch pearl rayon around the entry hole. Surround the nest with 7mm ribbons stitched in single edge ruching. Finish by adding beads.

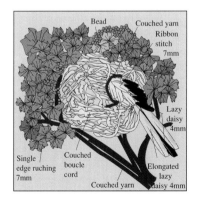

Square 5

Sketch tree branches and the outline of birds. Sew the birds first, using 4mm ribbons and the fern stitch. Sew beads in place for the eyes.

Tails are formed with the elongated lazy daisy. Sew the branches by couching pearl rayon in place. Leaves are created with the ribbon stitch using 7mm ribbon.

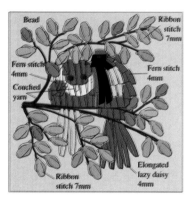

Square 6

Trace outline of the bird house. Form roof by couching 9mm Cottonaire© ribbon and boucle cord in place. Create the entry hole using the fern stitch with 4mm black ribbon. Draw the branch and stitch it by couching yarn in place. Create bird feet and beak by using elongated

lazy daisy stitches and couched pearl rayon. Use a bead to resemble an eye. Add 4mm lazy daisy leaves and finish with beaded berries.

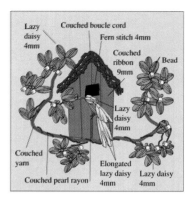

Square 7

Trace branches and couch pearl rayon in place. Using 4mm ribbons, create the bird body with the fern stitch. For bird tail, use an elongated lazy daisy stitch. Add bead to resemble an eye. The leaves are lazy daisy stitches created with 4mm ribbon. Finish with beads.

Square 8

Draw the shape of the bird house and couch 9mm Cottonaire© ribbon in place. Couch strands of brown yarn for the roof, leaving several frayed ends at the top. Draw branches and couch brown yarn in place. The bird breast is formed with ribbon stitches of 7mm ribbon. Finish the body with elongated lazy daisy stitches. Couch pearl rayon for beak and add a bead for eye. Work leaves last, with a lazy daisy stitch and use 2mm ribbon.

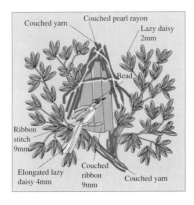

Square 9

Make the shape of the nest. Couch boucle cord and nubby cotton yarn in place. Work from the outside to the inside. Sketch the shape of the branches and couch yarn in place. Pictured bird is sewn over the nest. Create the breast of the bird with the chain stitch using

4mm ribbon. Form the head and body with ribbon stitches using 9mm Cottonaire© ribbon. The wings and tail are 4mm ribbon using the elongated lazy daisy stitch. The other bird is sewn the same way. Now use 7mm ribbon for the leaves, adding 4mm flowers with lazy daisies, and finish with the beads.

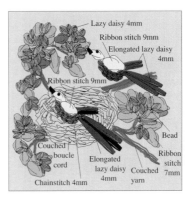

To finish picture, carefully stretch piece on stretcher bars. To prevent work from becoming distorted, it is important to keep the fabric on grain when stretching over bars and frame. Glass is not recommended as it will flatten embroidery. If it is necessary to protect your work from elements, try a shadow box type frame that sets the glass away from the picture.

QUICK PROJECT - PILLOW

MATERIALS

Linen or similar fabric - two 16"
    squares

Cotton or lining fabric (dark color) -
    one 14" square

Cording or piping - 1 1/3 yards

Thread: matching 50 or 60 weight
    thread, matching regular
    weight thread

Wing needle - size 100 or 120

Ribbons and Beads for select square
    (see "It's for the Birds"
    materials list)

Purchased pillow form - 12"

Border design ribbon: 2mm medium
    green, 7mm light green over-
    dyed

Border design beads - pink shades
    size 8/0

From 16" square of linen, pull threads according to fabric preparation instructions on page 59. Pull threads to create a 6" square inside an 8" square.

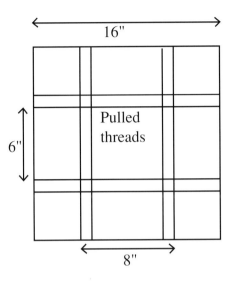

Sew hemstitching according to instructions on page 59.

Stitch embroidery according to instructions on pages 60 - 63 for chosen design.

The illustration is an example of a square and the border design.

Couched 2mm ribbon   Beads   Ribbon stitch 7mm

To finish pillow, trim embroidered linen to a 13" square. Stay on grain and center design. Trim dark colored cotton lining to 13" square. Baste lining piece behind embroidered square. Stitch cording or piping trim around the square. Hint: many trims are difficult to join and are visible if joined into a seam. For balance, make sure joint seams are on all four corners!

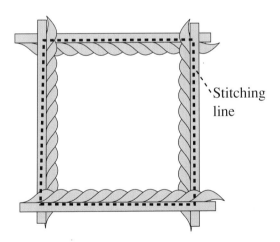

Stitching line

Trim, on grain, the other linen piece to a 13" square. Place linen piece right sides together with your embroidered square. Leaving one edge open, stitch around three edges and all four corners. After inserting the pillow form close the opening with a hand or whip stitch.

HEIRLOOMS

This purse is an excellent evening bag. It is perfect for a bride on her special day!

We used "color on color" for a soft, subtle appearance. This is also beautiful when worked in pastels or threads and ribbons to match "that perfect" outfit!

The Quick Project is designed as a cosmetic bag to be used inside the evening bag.

COLOR ON COLOR PURSE

MATERIALS

White Faille or Taffeta - 3/4 yard
Silk ribbon: 2mm, 4mm, 7mm - off
    white and ivory
Scalloped lace single edge (2 1/2")
    (see illustration) - 1 yard

Purchased Piping - 1 1/2 yards
One Purse Frame - Note: pictured
    purse frame is an antique,

check out your local antique or
thrift stores. Similar frames,
although new, are available
from Bag Lady Press, Lacis and
Ghee's (see resource list on
page 93)

CUT

From white Faille or Taffeta, cut four pieces, using the purse pattern on page 96. One front, one back and two lining pieces.

For insert between front and back, cut two 1" x 20" pieces fabric.

The initial embroidery was stitched on the lace only. Using an air soluble marker, mark in one inch from the edge of the lace. This is referred to as "hoop space." Measure 8 1/2" in from lace edge. This area will be embroidered.

Repeat, for the second piece. (Refer to illustration.)

Insert lace in hoop and following the illustration, stitch the lazy daisies with French knot centers, and the large flowers with ribbon stitches. Create loop stitches and end with a loose French knot in the center. In essence, you have re-embroidered the lace! Let the design of your lace dictate what type of flowers you will use and the exact placement.

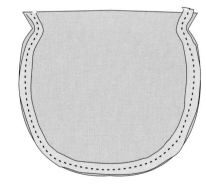

Attach the lace to your purse. Follow the markings on the purse pattern for lace placement. Use a small zigzag, and stitch the straight side of the lace on the lace placement lines. Stitch the ends in place.

Fill the resulting center oval space with flowers. Follow the diagram below or choose your favorites!

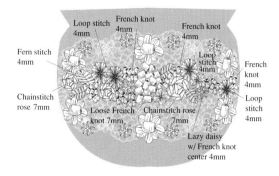

The back of the purse and the cosmetic bag are enhanced with one row of lace.

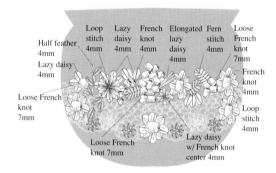

Purse assembly: Stitch piping in place on the front and back.

Use a 1/4" seam allowance and stitch the 1" x 20" piece of fabric between the front and back of the purse.

Construct the purse lining as before. Eliminate the piping.

Fold the raw edges of the top and press. Hand stitch the purse to the purse frame, stitching through the holes in the frame.

QUICK PROJECT COSMETIC BAG

MATERIALS

White Faille or Taffeta - 1/2 yard
Silk ribbon: 2mm, 4mm, 7mm,
off white and ivory
Scalloped lace, single edge,
(2 1/2") -1/4 yard

CUT

Two 5" x 13" pieces fabric

One 1" x 36" piece fabric (bias if possible)

Enhance with lace and ribbon embroidery following the Color On Color Purse instructions and the illustrations.

To form piping, fold the 1" x 36" strip in half and press. Keeping the raw edges together, stitch around the outside of the bag. Place lining and piped strip right sides together, and stitch using a 1/4" seam allowance. Leave a 3" opening in the center of one long side. Clip the corners, and turn right side out. Press, being careful not to flatten your embroidery. Fold in thirds, and stitch-in-the-ditch of the bias edge to form the sides of the purse. Fold down the embellished flap and secure with a snap.

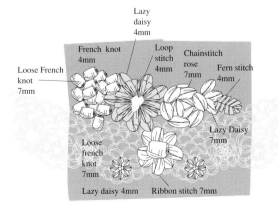

Those precious little babies, whether our children, grandchildren, or special friends are frequently the recipients of the fruits of our labors. This blanket or shawl can be worked on a ready-made woven blanket, or on individually pieced squares. Keep in mind that the ready-made woven blanket has squares already marked!

BABY BLANKET

Individual instructions for each square is included.

Numbers	Baby Carriage	Rabbit
	Bear	Rattle
Hand	Flower wreath	Foot
	Diaper pin	Duck
Lamb	Block	Alphabet letters

LAMB

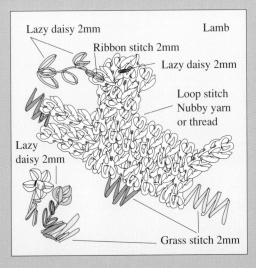

MATERIALS
Ready-made woven blanket
Ribbons: 2mm - light green, dark green, lavender, light yellow, dark brown
Nubby Yarn or Thread - white

Draw the shape of the lamb onto the blanket. Starting at the head of the lamb, work the loop stitch in rows to cover entire body. Use shorter loops in the head area and longer loops in body area. Work one ribbon stitch for mouth of the lamb. Create the illusion of the lamb eating one of the petals of the flower by making one lazy daisy stitch near the mouth. Drawing the loops taut, make one short lazy daisy stitch for an eye. The flowers are lazy daisy stitches. The leaves created with lazy daisy stitches and stems are couched. Work grass stitches to create grass.

BABY BLOCK

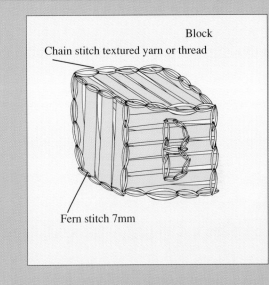

MATERIALS
Silk ribbon: 7 mm - aqua
Textured Yarn: multi-colored pastel or Heavy Thread

Sketch block shape onto the blanket. Working an elongated fern stitch, fill in a solid block area. Outline the edges and the letter "B" with a chain stitch.

ALPHABET LETTERS

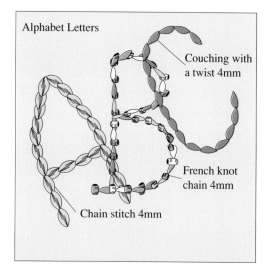

Alphabet Letters

Couching with a twist 4mm

French knot chain 4mm

Chain stitch 4mm

MATERIALS:
Silk ribbon: 4 mm - light turquoise, multi-colored, over-dyed, lavender

Sketch "A B C" onto the blanket. Create "A" with a chain stitch, starting at a low point and working an upside down "V". Work the horizontal line of letter "A" separately. Create "B" with a French knot chain stitch and the "C" using couching with a twist stitches.

DIAPER PIN

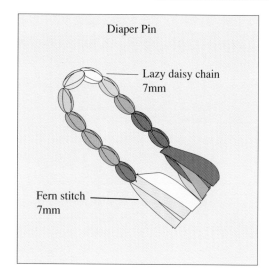

Diaper Pin

Lazy daisy chain 7mm

Fern stitch 7mm

MATERIALS:
Silk ribbon: 7 mm - multicolor

Draw the shape onto the blanket. Start at side of the loop of safety pin and make lazy daisy chain stitches creating the "wire" area of the pin. Cover the head of the pin by working the fern stitch.

DUCK

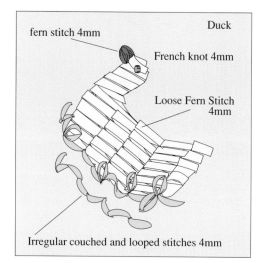

fern stitch 4mm

Duck

French knot 4mm

Loose Fern Stitch 4mm

Irregular couched and looped stitches 4mm

MATERIALS:
Silk ribbon: 4 mm - light yellow, medium yellow, brown, light turquoise

Trace the shape onto the blanket. Work a loose fern stitch starting at the top of the duck's head. Work the body of the duck in irregular rows with a loose fern stitch. Work up and down the body to cover shape. Create water with irregular looped and couched stitches. Make a French knot for the illusion of an eye. Make three fern stitches to create a beak.

HAND

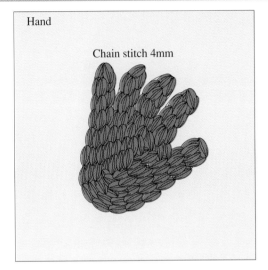

Hand

Chain stitch 4mm

MATERIALS:
Silk ribbon: 4 mm - medium brown

Draw shape onto the blanket. Starting at the base, on exterior of the hand, work chain stitch around outside. After completing outline, fill in the center working a circular shape in the palm of the hand. Working up and down, stitch fingers in vertical rows until center is filled.

FLOWER WREATH

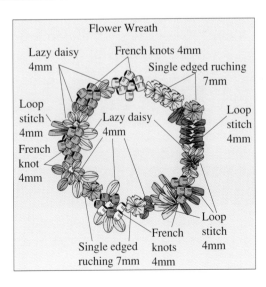

Flower Wreath

Lazy daisy
4mm

French knots 4mm

Single edged ruching
7mm

Loop
stitch
4mm

Lazy daisy
4mm

Loop
stitch
4mm

French
knot
4mm

Single edged
ruching 7mm

French
knots
4mm

Loop
stitch
4mm

MATERIALS:
Silk ribbon: 4mm - olive, light green, forest green, gold, lavender, yellow; 7mm - edge-dyed aqua, edge-dyed lavender, edge-dyed pink

Create flowers and leaves with loop stitches, single edge ruching, lazy daisy stitches, French knots and bouillon stitches.

FOOT

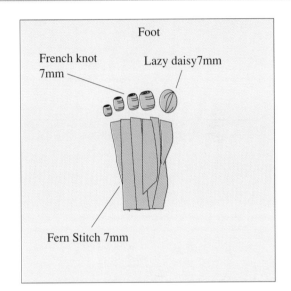

Foot

French knot
7mm

Lazy daisy 7mm

Fern Stitch 7mm

MATERIALS:
Ribbon: 7mm - light pink

Trace shape of the foot onto the blanket. Fill in foot area with elongated fern stitches. Use one lazy daisy stitch to create big toe (almost round). With progressively less rotations around needle to make them smaller, use French knots to create the other four toes.

BEAR

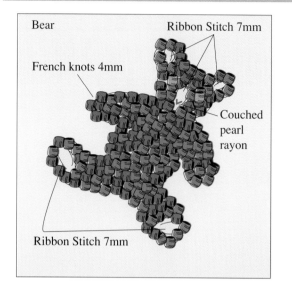

Bear

French knots 4mm

Ribbon Stitch 7mm

Couched pearl rayon

Ribbon Stitch 7mm

MATERIALS:
Silk ribbon: 4mm - dark and medium brown, light brown; 7mm - over-dyed tan/peach
Pearl rayon - red

Trace shape of bear onto the blanket. Make a ribbon stitch using 7 mm ribbon for the foot pads, nose area and ear linings. Stitch outline of the bear using dark and medium brown shades of ribbon. "Carry" the color that is not being used by bringing a second ribbon with one being used for French knot. This places it in position to be used when necessary. Fill in body of bear with random rows of French knots. Create eyes with French knots using light brown ribbon.

Create mouth by taking two close running stitches, by hand, using red pearl rayon.

RATTLE

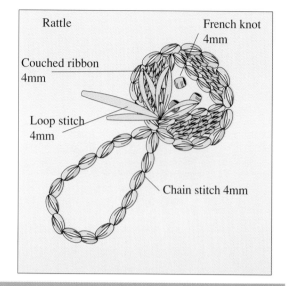

Rattle

French knot 4mm

Couched ribbon 4mm

Loop stitch 4mm

Chain stitch 4mm

MATERIALS:
Silk ribbon: 4 mm - yellow, aqua

Draw the shape of the rattle onto the blanket. Using one strand of each color and alternating sides, begin at the top of the rattle handle and work a chain stitch. Continue working around the perimeter of the body of the rattle. Edge triangle in yellow ribbon with a chain stitch. Fill in the open area, couching aqua ribbon. Create the eyes and mouth by stitching French knots. Stitch large loops for a bow at the meeting point of the handle and rattle.

NUMBERS

MATERIALS:
Silk ribbon: 4mm - lime green, dark teal, over-dyed lavender/gray

Draw the shapes on the blanket. Starting at top of the number "1," stitch a French knot chain. Working a looped stitch in a row, create number "2." Work the number "3" with a chain stitch.

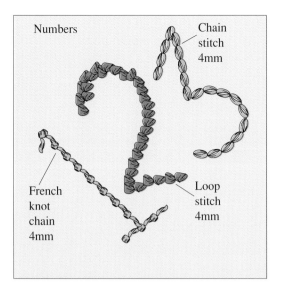

Numbers — Chain stitch 4mm — Loop stitch 4mm — French knot chain 4mm

BABY CARRIAGE

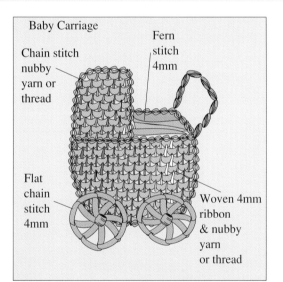

Baby Carriage

Chain stitch nubby yarn or thread — Fern stitch 4mm — Flat chain stitch 4mm — Woven 4mm ribbon & nubby yarn or thread

MATERIALS
Silk ribbon: 4mm - lavender, lavender over-dyed, light taupe
Nubby Yarn or Heavy Thread
Large eye needle

Draw the shape of the carriage onto the blanket. With 4 mm lavender work a basic woven basket technique. Lay the ribbon horizontally, and stitch down the ends only. Cover the carriage. Weave nubby thread in and out of the ribbon. A large eye needle makes weaving easy. Anchor ends of the nubby yarn. Stitch the blanket with a wide fern stitch. Create the carriage handle with a chain stitch. Work the chain stitch with nubby thread to outline carriage. Create the wheels, spokes and circular areas with a flat chain stitch. Finish with a French knot in the center.

RABBIT

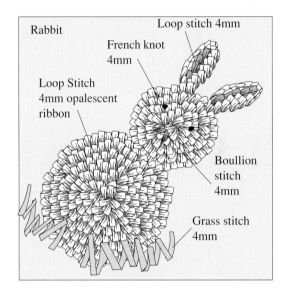

Rabbit — Loop stitch 4mm — French knot 4mm — Loop Stitch 4mm opalescent ribbon — Boullion stitch 4mm — Grass stitch 4mm

MATERIALS
Silk ribbon: 4 mm - over-dyed light green, mauve, black,
Braid or Yarn: 4mm - opalescent

Sketch the rabbit pattern onto the blanket. Begin at the ears with opalescent braid, making loop stitches around outside of ears. Fill in ear with a second row of loop stitches. Using mauve silk ribbon, work loop stitches for center row. Work the body and head of the rabbit with circular rows of loop stitches. Create two French knots, using black silk ribbon, for eyes. To form mouth position two bouillon stitches in an inverted "V" shape. Work the grass stitch to create grass.

What is more special than a new baby in our lives? Whether we are a mother, a grandmother, an aunt or a special friend, the birth of a baby is a wonderful event.

A Christening dress is for a special baby as well as generations of babies to come!

Learn to adapt a basic baby dress pattern, a few yards of coveted fabric, lace and silk ribbon into an heirloom to be treasured for generations.

No babies in your life? Create a Quick Project Potpourri Bag on page 79.

CHRISTENING DRESS

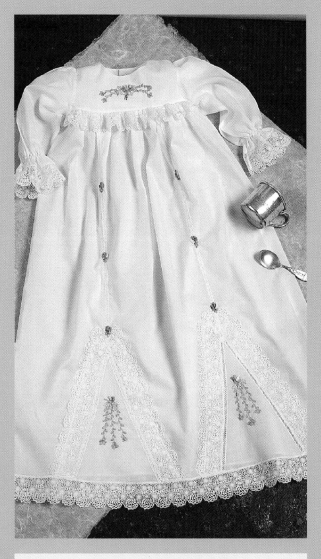

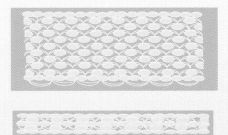

Commercial pattern - basic baby dress with yoke and puffed sleeves

Imported or domestic 100% cotton batiste - 4 yards

Edging lace (2") - 5 yards

Insertion lace (1/2") - 3 yards

Threads: regular sewing thread, white 60 weight embroidery thread, white pearl rayon

Silk ribbons: 2mm - pale green
4mm - pale peach
7mm - baby blue, pale pink and pale yellow

Ribbon floss - pale blue, pale pink, pale yellow

PREPARATION

Pre-wash all fabric and laces, especially if the finished dress will be machine washed. Press fabric and laces with an iron. Spray starch the fabric to make it easier to work with and help it stay "fresh."

Using a wash out marker, trace off the front yoke pattern onto a piece of fabric. Fabric piece should be large enough to fit in the hoop. Lengthen the skirt pattern pieces to 27".

Cut back yokes, sleeves, facings and any remaining pattern pieces.

Cut out the skirt and mark the areas for lace insertion, following the diagram on page 78.

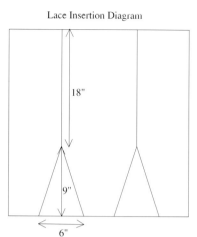

Lace Insertion Diagram

18"

9"

6"

An easy way to sew lace insertion! Set sewing machine for a zigzag with a 2 width and 2 length. Lay the insertion lace on the marked lines and zigzag each edge. At this point in the project, don't worry about the ends. Use one of the following lace insertion techniques; 1) Carefully cut away fabric from behind the lace using a small, sharp embroidery scissors. Be careful not to cut into the lace. This gives an authentic, "inserted" appearance; 2) Leave the fabric behind the lace. This is sturdy and "holds up" through years of wash and wear.

Begin embroidery by setting machine for ribbon embroidery as instructed on page 12. Sketch embroidery pattern for the yoke. Stitch the vines first, adding buds at the end of the vines. Stitch daisy's using ribbon floss. Work stems with pearl rayon. Finish with the bouillon roses and leaves.

Following the diagram, sketch embroidery

design and follow the previous instructions. Stitch details on the bottom of the skirt.

Skirt bottom

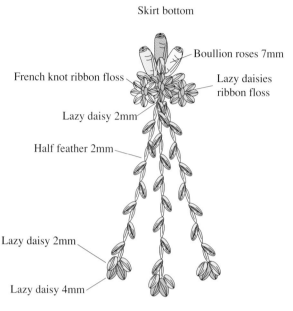

Boullion roses 7mm

French knot ribbon floss

Lazy daisies ribbon floss

Lazy daisy 2mm

Half feather 2mm

Lazy daisy 2mm

Lazy daisy 4mm

Read pattern instructions, note the following changes and assemble dress.

Before joining the yoke to the skirt, measure the bottom of the front yoke. Cut edging lace 2 1/2 times this length. Gather edging lace to fit front yoke and baste it in place. Repeat for the back yokes.

On the outer edges of the bottom "triangle" insertions, stitch edging lace in place. At the top, fold the ends under to cover the raw edges of the insertion lace. Stitch the edging lace around the bottom.

Stitch the rosebud clusters on the top of the panel, at the bottom of the skirt. Add two more rosebud clusters above this at 5" intervals.

Rosebud cluster

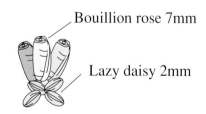

Bouillion rose 7mm

Lazy daisy 2mm

Yoke

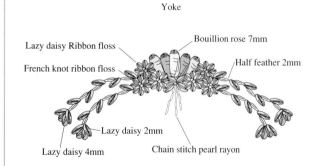

Lazy daisy Ribbon floss

Bouillion rose 7mm

French knot ribbon floss

Half feather 2mm

Lazy daisy 2mm

Lazy daisy 4mm

Chain stitch pearl rayon

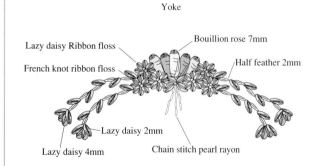

QUICK PROJECT - POTPOURRI BAG

This project is wonderful for a baby, a bride, your Grandmother or for yourself! Practice embroidery techniques on this potpourri bag, fill it with your favorite scent and enjoy!

From batiste, cut one 5" x 6" piece and one 5" x 2 1/2" piece. Trace the basket design and various flowers designs on remaining piece of fabric. Center design on 5" x 6" piece which will be cut later. Fabric must be large enough to fit in hoop.

Sew the lace in place following instructions on page 78. To achieve smooth curves, the edging lace may require "snipping" between motifs. Practice your ribbon embroidery skills! Explicit instructions follow, but feel free to use your favorite flowers.

Lazy daisy 4mm
Bouillion rose 7mm
Lazy daisy Ribbon floss
Edging lace
French knot Ribbon floss
Insertion lace

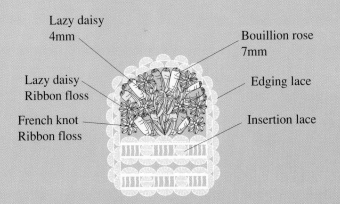

Begin potpourri bag assembly by trimming embroidered piece to 5" x 6". Place it WRONG sides together with the other 5" x 6" piece. Sew a French seam by stitching a scant 1/4" seam allowance along two sides and the bottom. Turn right sides together and carefully press the edges, being careful not to "flatten" the embroidery. Using a 1/4" seam allowance, enclose the raw edges by stitching along the same two sides and the bottom.

Construct the flap by pressing under 1/8" on the two 2 1/2" edges. Do the same for the 5" x 2 1/2" piece. Press under 1/8". Stitch in place. Fold right sides together and stitch. Open and press.

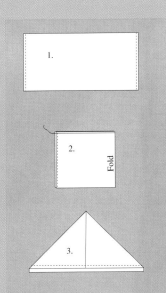

Attach flap to the embellished front. Use the above described French seam method. Stitch a tiny buttonhole on the flap and attach a tiny button on the bag back. The potpourri bag is complete!

Smocking, originally hand worked, is an age-old art. As with many traditional fiber art techniques smocking has been adapted to machine. The smocked dress project combines machine smocking with ribbon embroidery!

SMOCKED DRESS

MATERIALS

Commercial yoke/gathered skirt
    dress pattern
45" 100% Cotton or cotton/
    polyester blend broadcloth
    - as required on pattern
    plus 1/2 yard
Thread: matching regular sewing
    thread, contrasting rayon
    embroidery thread for
    decorative machine stitch
    (green in pictured project)
Iron-on stabilizer such as
    "Sulky's™" Totally Stable© -
    1 package
Silk ribbons: 4mm - apple green,
    bright blue, bright pink,
    purple

Traditionally, smocked fabric is gathered with a device called a pleater. If you don't have access to a pleater, call a local fabric shop specializing in smocking. Many shops pleat fabric at a minimal charge. Another option is to gather fabric with a sewing machine. Use a gathering foot, or sew a long basting stitch and pull the bobbin threads.

CUTTING

The dress front is cut after the smocking and decorative stitching are complete. Begin by cutting a length of fabric, to pleat or gather, for the front of the dress. Determine the length by measuring the length of the front yoke pattern piece and the length of the skirt. The combined measurement is the required length to cut for the dress front. Following the diagram, gather or pleat this length of fabric. Gathering or pleating stitches should be 1/2" apart and cover 9 inches.

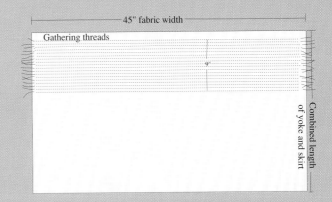

Cut the back bodice pieces, back skirt and sleeves. The front skirt pattern piece will not be used. After embroidery is complete, the front bodice pattern piece will be placed on top of fabric and cut. Instead of using any facing pieces, the neck is bound with self bias binding strips. Cut a bias strip 2" by 24" for the neck.

After gathering or pleating fabric, lay it out flat on the ironing board, and smooth it until it is wide enough to accommodate your bodice pattern piece. Distribute gathered stitches evenly across the width and keep pleats straight from top to bottom. Place a piece of "Totally Stable©" or other iron-on stabilizer on the wrong side of the gathering stitches. Press in place with your iron. Lay the front bodice pattern piece on pleated fabric and, using a wash-out or fade-away marker, trace off the bodice outline.

Mark off the position of decorative machine stitches and ribbon embroidery. Ribbon embroidered flowers are 2" apart. Following the diagram, mark a dot with a wash-out or fade-away marker. Connect the dots for machine decorative stitching lines.

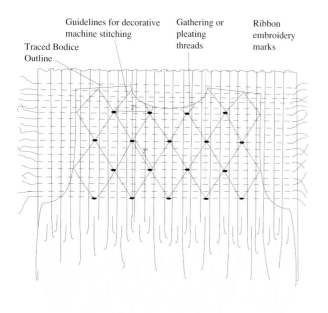

Guidelines for decorative machine stitching

Gathering or pleating threads

Ribbon embroidery marks

Traced Bodice Outline

Decorative machine stitching will be worked first. Thread your machine top and bobbin with rayon embroidery thread. Place an appliqué foot on the sewing machine and choose desired decorative stitch.

Because of thickness variations in fabric, close stitches do not "flow" evenly. Use an open stitch to allow the "give" required with smocked items. Stitch diagonally from dot to dot.

Set machine for ribbon embroidery following the instructions on page 12 in preparation of creating lazy daisies! Stitch lazy daisy leaves with green. Create flowers, adding French knots in the centers using pink, purple and blue ribbons.

Ready to assemble the dress? Check the lines by placing the bodice pattern piece on your embroidered front. Cut out the bodice, neck, shoulder, arms and side seams. **DO NOT CUT BOTTOM OF BODICE.** The skirt will naturally flow! Following individual pattern instructions, complete your dress.

Apply the bias binding to the neck edge by folding strip in half lengthwise. Press. Keeping the raw edges together, place the binding on the wrong side of the dress and, using 1/4" seam allowance, stitch. Trim the excess from the ends to 1/4". This allows enough to fold the raw edge and finish off the back neck opening. Fold under the 1/4" and press. Fold the binding over to the right side, press and stitch in place. Remove stabilizer from the underside of the dress.

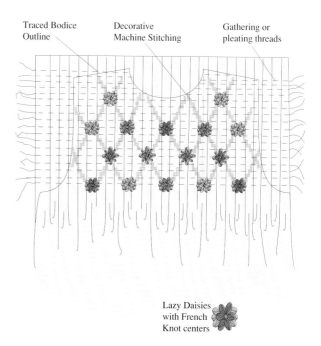

Traced Bodice Outline

Decorative Machine Stitching

Gathering or pleating threads

Lazy Daisies with French Knot centers

QUICK PROJECT - SMOCKED BONNET

MATERIALS

100% Cotton or cotton/polyester blend broadcloth - 1/4 yard

Totally Stable© or similar iron on stabilizer - 12" x 6" piece

Thread: green rayon embroidery thread (contrasting), regular sewing thread to match fabric

Silk ribbons: 4mm: apple green, bright blue, bright pink purple 1/8" - 1/4" double face satin or grosgrain ribbon

If necessary, trim your fabric. "Square-up" and make sure it measures 9" x 44". Roll hem one long edge by turning under 1/4" once, and then again. Straight-stitch in place. Hem the other casing edge by turning the raw edge under 1/4", then 1/2". Straight-stitch in place.

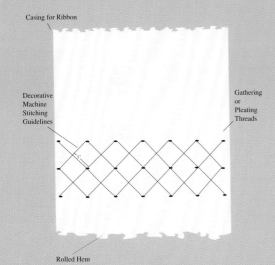

The rolled hem can be sewn on a serger.

Gather or pleat the fabric. The design is worked on the half near the rolled hem. Pull up gathers to measure 12". Straighten out the pleats or gathers and iron the Totally Stable© on the wrong side of the fabric.

Mark dots, according to decorative stitching diagram, with a fade away or washout marker. Mark dots at 1" intervals. Sew decorative stitches, and complete ribbon embroidery

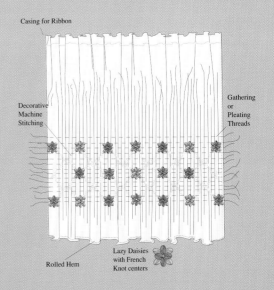

according to instructions. Run an 18" length of satin or grosgrain ribbon through the casing in the back of the hat. Cut the remaining satin or grosgrain ribbon in half and center on the embroidery. Stitch in place. Remove the stabilizer from the back of the bonnet.

BOILED WOOL

Create a boiled wool vest with the flavor of Austria and a spice that's yours alone! Following are guidelines for making boiled wool, color blocking and specifics of pictured vest. Personalize your vest by choosing your favorite colors, flowers and embellishments!

BOILED WOOL VEST

This boiled wool vest is embellished with ribbon embroidery and beads.

MATERIALS

Commercial vest pattern (without darts)
Lining fabric per pattern requirements
Three 100% wool sweaters - yellow, fuschia, red
Silk ribbon: 2mm - medium green, dark green; 4mm - bright blue, medium blue, purple, bright pink, light pink, bright yellow
7mm - medium green, dark green; boucle cord - purple, dark green
Threads: sewing thread to coordinate with sweaters
Beads: multicolored size 6/0 bright pink size 8/0

CREATING BOILED WOOL

Boiled wool has been in existence for centuries. Remember the time you washed a wool sweater and it shrunk? Through this mistake, you may have created boiled wool! Boiled wool has a wonderful thickness, density and texture not found in any other fabric.

The boiled wool vest and hat are projects which call for you to scour your drawers for old sweaters. Some sweaters have moth holes, or are out of date, but are too good to throw out! If you don't personally have wool sweaters that fit these categories, check with your Grandparents or visit your local thrift shops and tag sales. These sweaters don't have to be in great shape, they need only be made of 100% wool. They can be any size, type of wool knit or shape. Pictured are projects of rib knit, lightweight lambs wool single knit and a standard knit pullover.

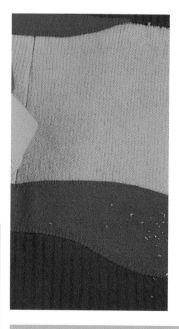

The pictured vest was created with three different sweaters; a red, a fuschia and a beautiful, bright yellow sweater. The washing and drying times varied between these in order to even out each different weight of wool.

EVEN OUT WOOL WEIGHTS

With regular laundry detergent, wash and dry each wool item one time in the washing machine. Use a hot water wash, with a cool rinse cycle (if available on your washing machine). If not, use hot wash and warm rinse. Dry on a permanent press cycle. This hot to cold process "shocks" the wool, and causes the desired shrinkage.

Study the results of the wash/dry process. The thickness of the wool types should be uniform in thickness and fairly stable, not thin or stretchy. The texture should be plush and thick, not soft and easily draped. The looser the knit in the original fabric, the more washings are required. Continue washing fabric individually until they are uniform in texture.

After desired texture is achieved, study fabrics for possible uses before cutting them apart! The ribbed section from the bottom of one sweater band was used in the boiled wool hat! The side seams of the original sweaters are in the center back of the pictured vest. The side seams are not visible because they "melded" together in the shrinkage process. Most seams in the original sweater will disappeared in the shrinkage process. Sweaters shrink to about half of the original size.

Choose a simple commercial vest pattern without darts, princess seams etc. Locate the vest pattern pieces. Only a front and a back pattern piece will be used. If facing pieces are included in the pattern, set them aside.

PREPARING SWEATERS

Shrunk sweaters are ready to cut! Cut open **one** side seam by cutting next to the seam on each sweater. Carefully cut the seams on the shoulders, sleeves and neck. **Don't cut the other side seam.** Lay out the bodies of your sweaters, and measure the width. Enough fabric is required to accommodate the width of the back of your vest.

PIECING

Workable fabric includes the body and two sleeves of each sweater. Piece them together to achieve sufficient fabric to cut a vest back, and two vest fronts. This is called **color blocking**!

Join straight edges. Create interest by cutting pieces into irregular shapes. To do this, lay them one on top of the other, and mark a curvy line on the top one. Pin through both layers, and cut them both at the same time. This will result in matching curves. A rotary cutter works well for cutting multiple layers.

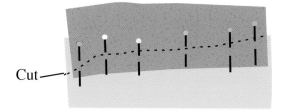

Pictured vest includes ribbon embroidery embellishment on most of the seams. Butt seams to join together. Place pieces side by side, and sew them with a zigzag, or bridging stitch. Place a scrap of lining fabric under the seams to give the stitches a foundation. Do not place right sides together and stitch, seams will be too bulky.

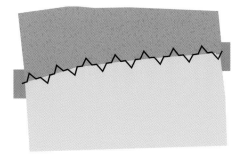

After you have created a piece of fabric, lay your vest back pattern piece on top, and cut.

Join the remainder of the sleeves together and cut the vest fronts.

SEWING

Sew the side and shoulder seams. To minimize bulk, press seams open and topstitch them flat.

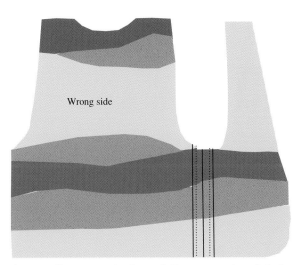

Wrong side

Assess the remainder of the sweater fabric and determine if you have sufficient to cut bindings. Bindings require 1 1/2" wide strips, of sufficient length to go around vest sleeves, front, back and neck. Purchase a fold-over binding if you find you don't have enough leftover.

EMBELLISHMENT

The various stitches are shown in the Stitches chapter on page 15. The diagrams below show suggested flowers and embroidery combinations. For additional flowers and combinations of stitches used to embellish, refer to "Ribbon Embroidery by Machine," published by Chilton; a division of Krause Publications, 1996. Flowers have been embellished with beads, adding a touch of sparkle and highlights in a way that is wonderfully three dimensional!

Sew beads in place while working ribbon embroidery. It is much more efficient to sew beads at this time, instead of going back after our embroidery is finished. When placing a bead, such as in the middle of a flower, stitch the bead in desired position and continue working your ribbon embroidery. For specific beading instructions, refer to page 29.

Silk ribbon was used throughout, unless otherwise indicated. The mm numbers are the width of the ribbon.

Flat lazy daisy 2mm
Bead
Lazy daisy 4mm
Flat lazy daisy 2mm
Lazy daisy 7mm
Couched boucle cord
Lazy daisy 4mm
Bead
Chainstitch rose 4mm
Bead
Chainstitch rose 4mm
Lazy daisy 2mm
Lazy daisy 7mm
Lazy daisy 2mm
Ruching 7mm
Bead
Ruching 7mm
Bead
Bead
Couched boucle cord
Lazy daisy 4mm
Bead
Lazy daisy 4mm
Bead
Bead
Lazy daisy 4mm
Single chain 7mm
Lazy daisy 2mm
Bead
Lazy daisy 4mm
Lazy daisy 4mm
Lazy daisy 2mm
Bead
Lazy daisy 7mm
Bead
Chainstitch rose 4mm
Lazy daisy 2mm

Silk ribbon was used throughout, unless otherwise indicated. The mm numbers are the width of the ribbon.

Chainstitch rose 4mm
Bead
Ribbon stitch 7mm
Bead
Feather stitch 2mm
Lazy daisy 4mm
Bead
Lazy daisy 4mm
Feather stitch 2mm
Lazy daisy 4mm
Ribbon stitch 7mm
Lazy daisy 4mm
Ribbon stitch 7mm
Feather stitch 2mm
Bead
Bead
Bead
Lazy daisy 4mm
Boucle cord
Lazy daisy 4mm
Ruching 4mm
Lazy daisy 4mm
Bead
Lazy daisy 4mm
Feather stitch 2mm
Half feather 2mm
Lazy daisy 4mm
Feather stitch 2mm
Lazy daisy 4mm
Chainstitch rose 4mm
Lazy daisy 4mm
Bead
Rusching 4mm
Lazy daisy 4mm
Bead
Boucle cord

BINDING

Finish vest by binding the edges using one of the two methods provided. There is no need to turn under edges. The shrinkage process in boiled wool prevents the edges from raveling.

METHOD ONE

Cut boiled wool remnants into 1 1/2" strips.

1. Using a regular straight-stitch, sew 5/8" from the edge around all edges to be bound.

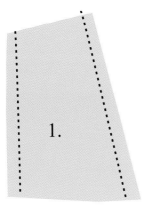

2. Thread sewing machine with invisible thread. On the wrong side of your vest, line up binding with the 5/8" guideline and zigzag in place.

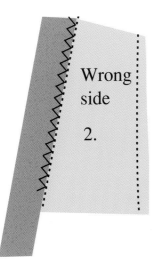

3. Fold the binding over to the right side. Steam press it in place, easing the binding around the curves. It is helpful to pin binding in place, however use caution not to sew over the pins.

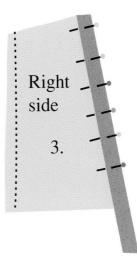

4. Sew binding in place on the right side of vest using a blanket stitch, zigzag, or straight-stitch. For emphasis, use a contrasting thread or a thread to match binding.

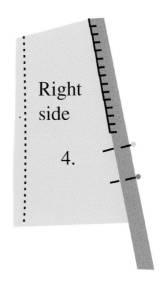

METHOD TWO

Purchased Binding - bias tape or very special woven braids.

Purchased binding has a finished edge and can be applied according to the boiled wool instructions. Or, it can be stitched in place, flat, turned over to the right side and hand stitched in place.

Enjoy your vest, and revel in the compliments you will receive!

Use your scraps to make a hat or if time is limited, use only one sweater. This is an excellent beginner project.

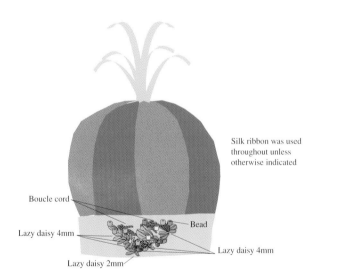

Silk ribbon was used throughout unless otherwise indicated

Boucle cord

Bead

Lazy daisy 4mm

Lazy daisy 4mm

Lazy daisy 2mm

Follow the Boiled Wool instructions on page 86. Use a commercial hat pattern or trace a favorite hat. Cut hat pieces and construct. Note diagram for embroidery stitches.

The hat tassel is made from boiled wool scraps. Cut scraps into strips of fringe, roll, and hand stitch in place.

RESOURCES

Build a ribbon collection or add to your current stock by visiting your local fabric, craft, quilt or yarn shops. Some shops will order needed supplies. If materials and supplies are not easily visible, ask for assistance. Explore and investigate every nook and cranny! Many supplies are available through mail order.

YLI Corporation

161 West Main Street
Rock Hill, SC 29730
customer service. 803-985-3100
orders. 800-296-8139

Nancy's Notions

333 Beichl Avenue
P.O. Box 683
Beaver Dam, WI 53916
customer service. 920-887-0391
e-mail.nzieman@aol.com
website. http://www.nancysnotions.com
orders. 800-833-0690

Clotilde Inc.

B3000
Louisiana, MO 63353
customer service. 800-545-4002
fax. 800-863-3191 (credit card orders only)
orders. 800-772-2891

Quilter's Resource, Inc.

P.O. Box 148850
Chicago, IL 60614
customer service. 800-676-6543
fax. 800-216-2374
orders. 800-676-6543

Andrew's Company

attn: Marie Duncan
1016 Davis
Evanston, IL 60201
customer service. 847-866-9595
e-mail. andrewsewco@earthlink.net
orders. 800-870-0404

Bag Lady Press

P.O. Box 2409
Evergreen, CO 80437-2409
customer service. 303-670-2177
fax. 303-670-2179
e-mail. baglady@baglady.com
website. http://www.baglady.com
orders. 888-222-4523

Ghee's

2620 Centenary Blvd #2-250
Shreveport, LA 71104
customer service. 318-226-1701
fax. 318-226-1781
e-mail. ghees@softdisk.com
orders. 318-226-1701

Lacis

3163 Adeline Street
Berkeley, CA 94705
customer service. 510-843-7178
fax. 510-843-5018
e-mail. staff@lacis.com
orders. 510-843-7178

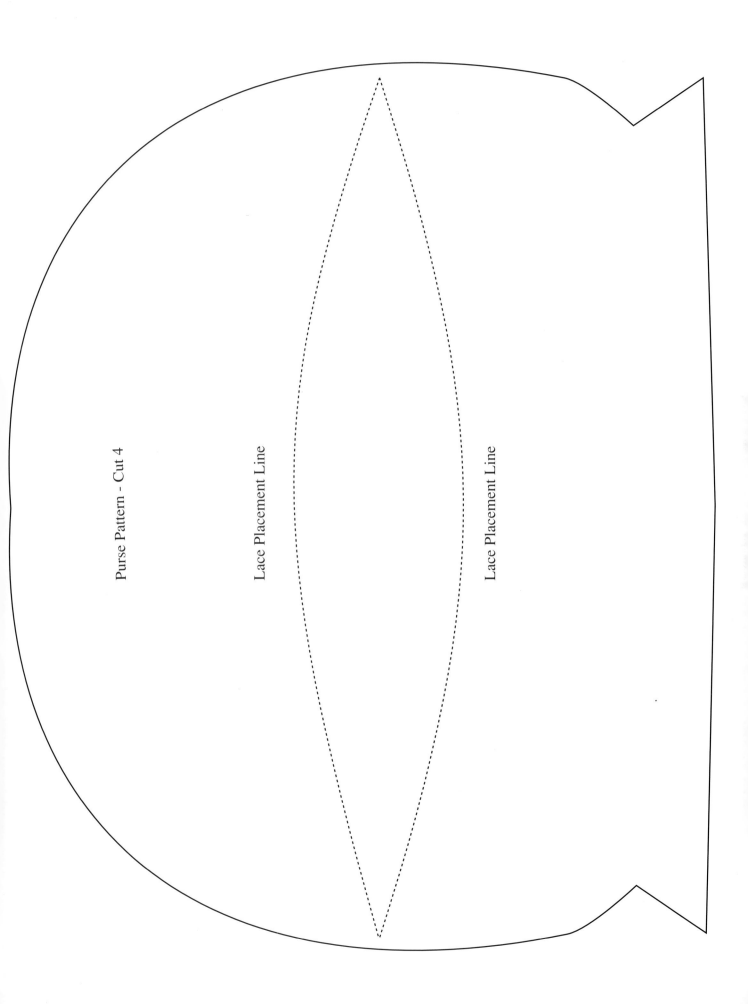

Purse Pattern - Cut 4

Lace Placement Line

Lace Placement Line